Living in the Space of Light

LIVING IN THE SPACE OF LIGHT

Dear Madeleine

Your inner light is a living vibrancy and an inspiration to do creatively beautiful and loving things.

Love

CAARNA

René

© 2012 Caarna

All rights reserved.

ISBN-13: 9781548240165
ISBN-10: 1548240168

To my husband, Peet, and my children, Alicia, Roxanne, Petrus; their partners, Bernard and Jessica; and my gorgeous grandchildren, Wouter and Ewald. You keep me grounded, and our strong bonds of love inspire me to find love in everything and everywhere. I am truly blessed to be surrounded by your light. Thank you.

Rene' Geldenhuys

CONTENTS

Introduction · ix

1   Let There Be Light · 1
2   The Natural Order of the Universe · · · · · · · · · · · · · · ·10
3   Good Vibrations ·16
4   A Touch of Love ·23
5   Every Moment Counts ·35
6   Gratitude ·41
7   The Balancing Act · 44
8   Diamonds Are Forever ·57
9   The Alchemist ·65
10 A Christed Being ·74
11 Sacred Space ·79
12 The Garden of Stars · 86
13 Bad Things Happen to Good People · · · · · · · · · · · · · ·110
14 Enlightening Lightning ·118
15 To Breathe Is to Live ·128
16 To Be in Touch · 136
17 The Path of Least Resistance · · · · · · · · · · · · · · · · · · ·143
18 Fear = Self-Induced Suffering · · · · · · · · · · · · · · · · · · ·146
19 Be Happy ·153
20 The Sound of Your Song ·156
21 Plant the Garden of Your Soul · · · · · · · · · · · · · · · · · ·165

Reference ·167

INTRODUCTION

HUMAN POTENTIAL IS infinite. Your potential has no limits. The inner soul of each person is a light that is ready in potential for emergence and expression. Light is the phenomenal aspect of consciousness, meaning that consciousness and light are two sides of the same coin. Light carries consciousness, just as consciousness carries light. When light is emerging, consciousness is also emerging. Light emerging from the depth of our being is so mysterious that no exact definition can be given to it. Little wonder that Einstein once said: *For the rest of my life I want to reflect on what light is.*

Light illuminates consciousness, light is a living vibrancy. Light has a vibrant energetic quality and an uplifting quality. It inspires the heart and the will. Now we are getting to the mysterious nature of this inner light. It has a quality of will to it, especially a will to do something good, righteous, loving, and creatively beautiful. So light gives us an energetic vibrancy and inspiration to do creatively beautiful and loving things.

Light eliminates darkness. It eliminates any darkness of unhappiness, sorrow, or depression. It eliminates anger, jealousy, and hatred. Light eliminates all kinds of darkness in our psyche. This is the healing quality of spiritual light. It also eliminates the darkness of selfishness and ignorance. Selfishness is dark because it encloses a person into a self-absorbed and self-narcistic cocoon. Ignorance is dark because it cannot see beyond the small cave in which it is enclosed. So, both the selfish and the ignorant need to step out from their enclosed cocoons or caves, in order to see beyond their encapsulated reality.

This quality of eliminating darknesses and obstacles, is the illuminating quality of light – which brings sudden awakening and a greater expansion of consciousness. It has a quality of sincerity and truth to it. Also, it has a quality of caring and love to it.

Studies of the brain and the processes of perception have revealed that we do indeed construct our own experience of reality, and that this personal reality is very different from the external physical reality. In physics, space and time have been demoted from their absolute status. They are relative to an observers point of view. In their place we find the absoluteness of light. The speed of light is a universal constant, and so is the quantum of action encapsulated in a photon. For a photon traveling at the speed of light, as all photons do, time and space disappear. In some strange way, light seems to lie beyond both space and time – and, since it has no mass, beyond matter too.

Physical light that is perceptible and filling our world is really a physical reflection of the light of consciousness. Divinity is being conscious of itself.

Closer to the *Source of all Light* is greater order and intelligence, and further away is greater disorder and ignorance. All things in the universe have the latent Divine Light, no matter how far from the *Source of all Light,* yet the further things have smaller realisations of this latent Light - so they are more engrossed in their smaller concerns. The closer one is to the *Source of all Light,* the more realisation one has. The great path is to come closer to the Light; thereby realising and actualising more of the Light.

All creation is effused with Divine Light. Any part or being of creation holds a portion of the Divine Light, though all beings have an inherent potential to absorb or realise more and more of this.

Inner space consciousness and who you are in your essence are one and the same. In other words, the form of little things leaves room for inner space. It is from inner space, the unconditioned consciousness itself, that true happiness, the joy of being, emanates. To be aware of little, quiet things, however, you need to be quiet inside. A high degree of alertness is required. Be still. Look. Listen. Be present.

There is another way of finding inner space: Become conscious of being conscious. Say or think "I Am" and add nothing to it. Be aware of the stillness that follows the I Am. Sense your presence, the naked, unveiled, unclothed beingness. It is untouched by young or old, rich or poor, good or bad, or any other attributes. It is the spacious womb of all creation, all form. The self is present throughout the world and present within us. The self is through us and in front of us. The one self is who we really are, and it is the one self who experiences life - through this body and this mind called 'myself'.

Understand reality as three-fold: the level of pure light-consciousness-spirit, the level of thought, and the level of physical manifestation. If we consider creative possibilities, light-consciousness can create thought, and thought can then create physical manifestation. Reversely, physical forms can dissolve back to just thought, and thought can dissolve back to pure consciousness or light. The possibility then is that material form can dissolve back into its essential light energy, and then be re-created in a new form.

The light that we experience in the world is really consciousness reflecting back on itself. Thus, all light that is experienced both inwardly and outwardly is really a reflection of the pure divine consciousness. We know that everywhere around us is the reflection of pure divine consciousness. when we look at the world we see light reflecting everywhere and we see forms. The world of our outer experience is a world of forms, particular forms that we perceive. These forms are all made of light, their essential substance is light. This is light contracted into a form. The whole outer experience is only possible because of the inner reality of consciousness.

Space is not the mountain or the horizon outside there, as any localized object is a mere content of space. Likewise, all the observable objects are just contents of consciousness, not consciousness itself, as this is in fact the 'space of awareness' containing all experiences, all perceptions, and all the attempts to understand and rationalise them.

At the dimension of actual space, there are distinct points within the space. In other words, once there is actual space, there are a multiplicity of distinct points within that space. If we imagine an actual space where there is still nothing else but light, where the whole space is filled with light, then we can understand how there is light at every point in that space Each point is the same light as any other point, though each point is still distinct in itself from the other points. That is, in an actual space (where there is spatial area) we can visualize the possibility of being at one point called 'here' and looking around at other points 'over there'. So there are these distinct points in the great space and at each point is a unique perspective on how the whole space looks from that particular vantage point. Each point would have its own unique perspective on the whole space, yet each point is, nonetheless, a point of light or a point of awareness. Each point is 'looking' around at the space or at the other points in space from its unique perspective; and yet, each point has the same essential awareness, the same fundamental property of 'looking', or the same essential 'light of consciousness'.

The more elevated or purified our level of consciousness the more refined and penetrating our perception. That is why the purest individuals in our histories have also been the wisest and most perceptive, capable of seeing not only into the human heart, but into other dimensions.

Consciousness is not the mind or the senses. Consciousness utilizes the mind, heart, and senses to perceive, but can perceive levels of existence that are beyond our mind, heart, and physical senses. Consciousness is the means to ascend higher. This is always accomplished by awakening and perceiving more by means of the purification of the individual.

The light goes on when I open my mind, neurones are firing -
illuminate truth. What once was dark can now be seen. Not
always a comfortable place to be.
The pulse, the heartbeat, the breath of life is mine when I lay
with my head on the chest of the Source. I feel the love that
conquers all.
Let my heart be opened, let it be touched by the trees and the
wind
and the sun on my back.
Every perfect form of life bathed in Light. The wonder of
Creation takes my breath away. The order, the structure, the
blueprint of creation, a constant throughout the Universe.
Earth, water, fire and air constantly moving, seeking balance
for perfection they care.

LIVING IN THE SPACE OF LIGHT

*Where in this space do I stand? Enlightenment understands
what consciousness is, the search is turned within.
Self care, self love - to find the light within.
Miss not one moment to capture the perfection of what is.
Focus on each construction of the mind, bind the memories in
a file.
To know my desires, strengths, weaknesses and fears.
I own them, they belong to me. For with them I will manifest
whatever comes to me.
God give me courage to take responsibility for my very own!
Live life with an open heart, if anything seems impossible add a
touch of love
There is always so much to be grateful for, even if we struggle to
find balance in a world that seems hostile, cruel and cold.
Express gratitude for the good and the bad, it transforms to an
extra-ordinary life.
Thank You for every point of light in my space.
Forever reminded of the path of intense pressure and heat the
diamond had to endure, to eventually break through the surface
of the earth and become the strongest and most brilliantly
shining substance known.
It is the path to become a brilliantly shining gem in this world.
To be a beacon of light takes extra cut and polish for more
delight.
I reach enlightenment if I walk in the light
Use the tools gifted with a diamond bathed in violet light.
Bring balance wherever I go and raise the vibration
Turn on the magic in the space of light!*

*Christ came to show the way- stand and walk in sacredness.
Have courage to find Christ within. Walk in truth and fear no
ridicule*

CAARNA

God knows. I know. I am.
Create beautiful gardens filled with light when I walk through
the labyrinths of life. I shine my light so that I can see and in it
are so many blessings for all,
not just for me.
Sit at my table, I have prepared a feast
Come relax, find refuge to the harshness of life
Inside of me I have found the diamond that shines so bright, it
can not be dimmed,
It will forever be light
We breathe the same air, we drink the same water to keep us in
life.
We walk the same earth, we share the same light, for eons of
years
Those before me and with me and after me all the same
Just different colours of the same White Light
I reach out to touch to know I exist. Give and receive support.
Please hold me, I can not do this on my own
In the comfort of togetherness we trust. See, there is no need for
fear.
We know all is well and so it will be if we walk on the path
that has been cleared.
Thunder and Lightning! Sound to Light. Brighter and brighter,
shines the light.
Happy we sound when we sing and laugh out loud, through the
voice we resonate. As One we plant the garden.
Bring on- Heaven to Earth!

—CAARNA

1

LET THERE BE LIGHT

WHEN I WATCH old home movies of my childhood, I realise I was a peculiar child. *Strange, odd, funny, curious, weird, uncanny, atypical,* and *unusual* describe my looks and behaviour. Over the years I got used to receiving a curious look from family, friends, or strangers. It did not faze me too much because I knew I was different. I am destined to be different.

I could often answer questions that amazed people around me and have no idea myself how I knew anything about it in the first place. I had correct answers to mathematical calculations without knowing the steps to get there. If people did not see my worth, I simply stepped forward and showed them that I could do exactly what they wanted.

I remember the excitement, as a six-year-old grade-one learner, to hear the school was going to present a play. I sat on the stage while the teachers called the names of children who got roles and was absolutely stunned when they did not call my name. I sat with the other kids with green and brown, who supposedly were the grass and trees, and watched a beautiful petite blond girl, who was supposed to be a cornflower, walking to the front of the stage, swaying in the wind and bowing to the audience. She was so nervous, and I had never seen a scared flower, so next time we practised, I got up with her and held her hand, and when we bowed she gave me a bright smile. For the first time, she looked like a flower!

The teachers were stunned and looked at each other with big eyes, putting their heads together to quietly converse. The next time we practised, I got up with her again, and I saw how her eyes sparkled—she really was like a flower now! I was so happy that I became a flower too.

My mom was called in and handed a parcel with the most beautiful blue fabric and net for my cornflower costume. I expressed my gratitude by playing the cutest cornflower anyone could ever imagine.

As a young child, I was able to pull myself out of the world and observe how life played out around me. I was a loner till the age of about ten. Making friends was difficult, probably because I was floating around in the clouds most of the time. I later became more grounded and allowed myself to become part of this world. After that I made wonderful friends, and we shared the ups and downs of puberty and made lasting and loving memories together.

From a very early age, I needed to be alone and isolated. I often sat inside my cupboard, trying to get used to the dark. One day I found that my body could shine its own light, so I sat there for hours, shining my light till it wasn't dark in the cupboard anymore.

Later I found I did not need to sit inside my cupboard to make my light shine. It felt different to let it shine in the light, but it made me very happy, so I did it silently around my family and friends and saw it made them happy too. When I got a bit older, it was a natural progression to shine my light when there was fear or a crisis or when someone was fighting at home or at school.

After all the years of practicing in my dark cupboard, my body knew to switch its light on by just thinking about it. I learnt I could change people's moods or make things easier. As a child it was the most natural thing to do, with no intention to manipulate or to exercise my power over others. I simply did it to make the difficulties of the world easier. Eventually, in my teenage years, I gave my light to wherever I felt the need for love, compassion, or forgiveness.

I thought everyone else did the same. When I shared it with my brother, he looked at me with big eyes and said, "You do *what?*" I quickly shut my mouth and never shared that bit of information with anyone else until recently.

LIVING IN THE SPACE OF LIGHT

Sharing my light was the most natural thing for me to do, and I did it when I felt the need to do so, no questions asked, no debates or doubts. I just did it. As an adult I often found myself travelling to different places with a sense of knowing there was work to be done. Often it was just shining my light on towns or public places like schools or hospitals as we passed them on the road; other times we were stuck in a queue or in traffic if I needed more time, so I just allowed the light to flow out of my body to light up everything around me. I felt a deep sense of appreciation or gratitude for the gift.

I did not understand the value of gratitude yet and the ability it had to bring transformation, although my soul knew it well. Sharing my light was an effortless deed, which I mostly forgot about afterwards. It never sucked energy out of me but rather energised me. Every time I did it, I could feel the frequency of my own energy rising without knowing what was really happening. It was all a natural and effortless process that unfolded more than a conscious effort to make a difference. In a way, I did the process backwards because by the time I became conscious, I already had the tools to practise mindful living and to raise my own frequency.

I chose to follow a healing career at the age of six, when my father was involved in a mining accident. He needed months of intensive rehabilitation, and I often sat and watched while the physiotherapists were busy with him.

"That's what I want to do when I grow up," I used to say.

I never doubted my choice and worked hard at keeping the passion for my career alive by studying many different approaches, always searching for something that would make sense of how the body really works and what is needed for it to heal itself.

The study of acupuncture opened a whole new world to me, although I was so scared to follow that road. In the '90s it was still frowned on to practise any form of Eastern medicine in South Africa. I had long conversations with God before enrolling in the course. In the end, I realised, we are all scared to offend God with what we do. Apart from all the scientific knowledge I gained, it opened my mind to think outside the box, and I learned we could never offend God, no matter what we do. God is so much bigger than we can ever imagine! It is impossible to offend God.

We are not born with manuals on how to make this thing called life work. Knowledge of the laws of the Universe and how to apply them in life is probably the closest that we can get to having a manual.

Life is a journey of trial and error, of exploring, of experiencing to find our truth. We find our truth by travelling, observing how different people live, reading, watching movies, talking to people, collecting information, processing information, feeling compassion, putting ourselves in someone else's shoes, and asking ourselves how we would have handled a situation. We form an opinion about a situation, to make us understand better. You become aware of your own life, your upbringing, your cultural and religious beliefs. Compare it to what others experience, and start questioning what you were made to believe.

Finding your truth is a process of collecting information, processing it, testing if it agrees with you, much like trying foods you have never tasted— some you immediately spit out, others you just don't care for, and some you chew and roll around in your mouth to savour the taste.

Finding your truth is going through the whole process, exploring everything, keeping only what you like, and using it a lot until you find something that resonates with your being, till one day there is a definite *click* in your brain, and the piece of the puzzle fits in, and you can see better what the bigger picture looks like. There is a knowing within you that this belongs to you. From that moment on, you no longer have to look for other pieces that may fit into that specific part of the puzzle of life.

The challenge here is to realise we are all on our own journeys of finding our own truths. Some think they are good as long as they stay mainstream or part of the herd; they follow what others tell them to believe. Some are forced by circumstances of life to look at the puzzle from a different angle. Others are natural loners and don't want to be part of any group; they find their own paths. Some are forever searching to find meaning in life and will try many avenues to find their truths. Not one of these is better than another. They are simply experiencing life in their own unique ways. We must respect each other for where we stand in our journeys and allow one another the space and grace to walk through the labyrinth of life with noninterference.

We can still exchange information about the experiences of life because we all grow through that, but each person must be allowed to find his or her own truth at his or her own time and in his or her own way.

This is a process of going inside and not a search outside of self. It does not need the verification of others; it simply is your truth. Shining my light was simply my truth, and I did what I knew how to do and felt no need to share it or question it. It made me feel good. It taught me to hear the voice of God. It opened my heart and taught me compassion. It raised my consciousness. It opened me to receive the gifts of life.

I came into this world remembering a fraction of my true potential as a being of light and love. I used my gift without interference because I shared it with no one. There was no judgment or negative reaction from anyone about what I was doing, so it was the most natural thing in the world for me to do. It was the basis from where I could build my spiritual being without being classified as crazy.

I was a loner but never lonely because there was always a huge presence around me. God and His hosts of angels have always been there for me.

Truth resides in every human heart, and one has to search for it there, and to be guided by truth as one sees it. But no one has a right to coerce others to act according to his own view of truth.

—EDMUND BURKE

The truth is that until you know what you really want to say yes to, you will continue to say yes to everything else. Finding your own truth and questioning truth takes immense courage and is definitely not a process for the fainthearted. The path to realisation of inner divinity will require that you stand naked, stripped of all preconceived ideas of moral standards, religion, and upbringing to find your own truth that resonates deep within your heart and to find acceptance and knowledge of who you truly are.

Where do we start the journey? Most of us start looking at the outside world. We look at others, listen to what they have to say, what they feel, what they do. If their lives seem to work well, we spend time in their presence, mimic their behaviours and actions, join the same cultural and religious organisations. Some of us are driven by passion, so we dive in deep and try very hard to excel, to see change in our own lives and to know we are making a difference in others' lives. Others are just happy to find comfort in the company of like-minded souls and bask in the comfort of being accepted by a group. "If they think I am OK, I am happy that I am OK."

If we remain in our comfort zone for too long, we get bored, we question, we create drama to spice up life a bit. Group dynamics are played out—some love it, some hate it. We start looking around again. "Maybe this not where I need to be right now." Our radars go out, and we start scanning for a better location, a better role model, a more modern approach, and a fashionable group that stands out more. Some are satisfied they have found a comfortable place where they can be; for others, the search is a busy journey, and they are like little bees flying from one delicious flower to the next, stopping briefly but always searching for more of the sweetness of life.

All along we measure the outcomes with those who move around us who seem to know more than we do. At some point we wonder what we are missing. That is often when the search is turned inwards—when we ask the question "Is it possible I am responsible for this happening in my life?"

When we start looking at ourselves for reasons of dysfunction and misalignment, we start opening up to reveal the unfolding of all the complex but beautiful layers that make up the uniqueness of who we are. As we embark the journey of self-discovery and expand our awareness step by step, we stand in awe at the beauty of life as it unfolds from a rosebud to a beautiful, luscious, fragrant bloom.

Without self-knowledge, without understanding the working and functions of his machine, man cannot be free, he cannot govern himself and he will always remain a slave.

—G. I. GURDJIEFF

This is a process of going inside and not a search outside of self. It does not need the verification of others; it simply is your truth.

Seldom if ever will you find a person who knows everything about everything that is, was, and will be. Many have discovered pieces and fractions of it, but to see the big picture in its wholeness is simply not possible for most human beings.

It is astonishing that the truth lies within you, that it is always with you everywhere you go, and it waits to be discovered little by little, when the time is ready and when you are capable of comprehending the meaning that comes with it. External sources can guide you and show you the direction, but ultimately it takes no outward things to discover what always has been centred within you.

At some point in life, the answers that external sources provide will no longer satisfy the pursuer of truth. That's an inevitable stage during the pursuit of truth, but it also offers the opportunity to tune in to the stream of infinite wisdom that originates from deep within you. Following your intuition and listening to what your heart has to tell you is a fantastic way to discover what the wisdom of your higher self has to offer for you. Many of the journeys led by intuition will enable you to really do what you enjoy doing—something many describe as going with the flow of the Universe or walking on the path of God.

Encourage the stillness of the mind. When you are surrounded by silence and calmness, your mind engulfed in stillness, without expecting anything, intuition will make its voice heard. You already knew the truth a long time before you began searching for it. Insight will come to you when you are ready. If you are not ready for it, you won't accept it for what it is, until certain knowledge, experiences, and wisdom will prove you otherwise.

My motto is "life begins at the end of your comfort zone." The search for truth can be a very uncomfortable experience. The truth has to be discovered. It is up to you to discover piece after piece and to connect the dots in order to understand the so important bigger picture.

My journey of finding truth led me to dwell in the dark night of the soul. For two years I lived in a very dark place. I could not share it with anyone because I had to find my own way in the darkness. I felt vulnerable and empty. I had to let go of the foundation I had been brought up in. The *I* that existed up till then had feet of clay. Everything I lived by till then needed to be examined closely. It had to be taken apart and looked at under a magnifying glass till I could find the bits and pieces that resonated with my soul—my truth.

During this very dark period in my life, the movie *The Passion of the Christ* was doing the circuit, and I heard someone saying that you will really know why you are a Christian when you watch the movie. I had been brought up in a Christian home, but in the process of finding truth, I was stripped of my identity and did not know what I believed.

I took time off work one morning and sat nearly alone to see the movie, with only one other person with me in the cinema. I was waiting to be filled with passion for what I believed in, but instead I felt emptier than ever before. My tears spilled not for my passion to be called a Christian but because it was so frightening not to know what I believed in anymore. That was the lowest low I experienced, but it was also a turning point in my life. From there on I started picking up the pieces to build a stronger foundation of what resonated with my soul as truth. I am passionate to be a Christed being, to live a life in Christ's consciousness and by the example of Christ.

Listen to what the experts have to say, but also try to discover the opinions of those who oppose these specialists. Have in mind that people are sharing only *their* insights and *their* interpretations thereof, a lot of it highly influenced by their cultural and societal backgrounds, their education and belief systems, or those who pay them. If you are willing to educate yourself about a vast range of topics—science, religion, metaphysics, history, physics, astrology, ancient societies, and many more—you will spot similarities; you will see consensuses and accordances allowing you to grasp fractions of the bigger picture.

On your quest for the truth, you will come along many topics that seem to be just out there and so different from anything you have ever heard. You will hear people speaking about things our modern-day status quo of knowledge disputes the existence of. Yet many of those are sincere and regular people talking in the greatest detail of what they experienced or apparently know. In the end, it is important to investigate whatever topic resonates deep within you. Allow your heart to judge the legitimacy of what your brain considers to be pure science fiction. If you trust your heart, you will know who is sincere and who is outright fooling you.

Remain as open-minded as possible. Having a prejudiced mind-set about the whole world that surrounds you will hinder you from discovering new ideas and concepts, new approaches and mind-sets, and surprising realisations that provide you a further understanding of all that is. You're not doing yourself a favour by being biased only to conform to your personal beliefs and to be within a comfortable zone. Even if you think you discovered the truth, search further and further to widen your perspective. Leave no stone unturned in your search.

Be aware of the deception. It is important to understand there is deception, both knowingly and unknowingly, being spread everywhere you come across during your journey for the truth. There are those who do not teach the foundation of their inner truths and the wisdom gained from them but choose to be teachers of the concepts others create.

Listen to your heart, and you will know what resonates with you and what does not. You can listen to a thousand people, all of them presenting their own truths, but you will find your truth only within yourself. The only truth you will ever know in this lifetime resides deep within yourself.

2

The Natural Order of the Universe

WE PERCEIVE TIME as linear, with a beginning and an end, like a storybook. Our minds like to see order, starting with a "once upon a time" and ending with "they lived happily ever after."

How many of us have perfect stories to tell? Like the story of Job in the Bible, where he lost everything, including his wife and children, but it all ended well because he got a new wife and had more children and got back what he had lost. When I was a child that was the most horrifying story to listen to, so cruel. How can you be just as happy again when your wife and children are replaced like objects?

And so it is that we find ourselves in stories that are not so nice or are outright cruel, and we find ways to make this world a liveable place. We overcome so much loss, trauma, and stress, and we get right up and dust ourselves off and carry on. Something in us must know there is more to this life than hardship and struggle to make it worthwhile. How else will we find the courage to get up so many times?

The one thing that always inspires me to carry on is love. The love I feel radiating from God's creation, the love of being connected to everything else. The love I feel for being part of this world. I love to be alive! I treasure life and what it means to be alive. I basically love that I can feel that God is love.

We can endure so much pain, but we cling to life with all we have and in desperation. Our biggest fears are concerned with losing our lives. To be

LIVING IN THE SPACE OF LIGHT

separated from the ones we love, to end life on earth. Even if we say we are not scared of death, we are filled with a sense of relief and can feel a burst of adrenaline pumping when a life-threatening incident is overcome. Exhilaration and gratitude flush over us when we realise we are still alive.

Time and time again, we are pulled back to a central point of reference where we can align and balance and drink from the fountain of life—love.

Love is what sustains us; love is what we thirst for; love is what gives us hope; love is where we came from and love is where we strive to go. God is love and lovingly wove the golden strand throughout creation to keep us together as one. Although we often feel alone and deserted and in a very dangerous place, that constant pull towards our central point of reference will never let us go.

Life is a very beautiful piece of art that keeps on unfolding like a mandala. It maintains balance and structure by revisiting the central point of reference all the time. The point from where the drawing started originally. That first point of awareness of self, the exploration around self, seen as a circle. This is the story of geometry; of precision, alignment, balance; of checking in to the central point of reference to restore power, to inspire imagination, to find ways of creating beauty and form.

Sacred geometry is the basis or the blueprint of God's creation. The order and structure in creation is of mathematical precision, like music. There are specific formulae that have proved to be sustainable in the process of creation, and these numbers or notes are used to form the basis of new creations.

Everything in the universe is constantly moving in circular patterns. The world is in constant motion. It has no off days. It never gets tired. The billions of stars we admire on a clear night that seem motionless to the naked eye are moving at colossal speeds. Every star is a sun with its own ring of planets. The stars and the satellites circling round them also revolve on their own axes and participate in the turning of the whole galaxy around its axis. Various parts of the galaxy have different cycles. Our galaxy moves in relation to other galaxies. And there is no end to these whimsical courses of the universal roundabout.

At a certain stage in their evolution, some stars explode and flare up like huge cosmic fireworks. Our sun is a blazing hurricane. Its whole surface is

— 11 —

in a state of bubbling, erupting agitation. Colossal fiery waves pass over the turbulent solar surface. Huge fountains of flame—the protuberances—spurt to heights of hundreds of thousands of kilometres. The gigantic streams of internal heat that come to the surface are poured forth into space in the form of radiation.

Motion is the mode of existence of matter. To *be* means to be in motion. The world is integrating and disintegrating. It never attains ultimate perfection. Like matter, motion is uncreatable and indestructible. It is not introduced from outside but is included in matter, which is not inert but active.

Motion is self-motion in the sense that the tendency, the impulse, to change state is inherent in matter itself: it is its own cause.

Scientists today take for granted the idea that the Universe operates according to laws. All of science is based on what author James Trefil calls the principle of universality: "It says that the laws of nature we discover here and now in our laboratories are true everywhere in the universe and have been in force for all time."

As scientists record what they observe, most often they are not using just words and paragraphs. The laws of nature can be documented with numbers. They can be measured and computed in the language of mathematics. The greatest scientists have been struck by how strange this is. There is no logical necessity for a Universe that obeys rules, let alone one that abides by the rules of mathematics.

The speed of light measures the same 186,000 miles per second, no matter if the light comes from a child's flashlight or a star that's galaxies away. Mathematically, there is an exact speed of light that doesn't change.

Physicist Paul C. Davies comments:

> ...to be a scientist, you had to have faith that the universe is governed by dependable, immutable, absolute, universal, mathematical laws of an unspecified origin. You've got to believe that these laws won't fail, that we won't wake up tomorrow to find heat flowing from cold to hot, or the speed of light changing by the hour. Over the years I have often

asked my physicist colleagues why the laws of physics are what they are? The favourite reply is, "There is no reason they are what they are—they just are."

These Universal Laws can be compared to the very deep root system of a tree buried underground. The ordinary eyes cannot see the roots, yet they have so much influence on the tree because without them, the tree cannot exist.

The Law of Divine Oneness is the first of the twelve Universal Laws, and it helps us to understand that in this world we live in, everything is connected to everything else. Every thought, word, action, and belief of ours affects others and the Universe around us irrespective of whether the people are near or far away—in other words, beyond time and space.

The Law of Vibration states that everything in the Universe vibrates, moves, and travels in circular patterns. The same principle of vibration in the physical world applies to our feelings, desires, thoughts, dreams, and will. Each sound, thought, or thing has its own unique vibrational frequency. When you hear people say "like attracts like," they are actually referring to how a vibrational energy can resonate with or is attracted to the same or a similar vibrational energy. This is the reason why what others do or say affects us directly or indirectly.

However, if you are not happy with your current vibration, you will need to make a conscious choice to focus your energy more on positive emotions and less on negative emotions in order to raise your vibration higher, beyond the one you do not want in your life. If you do not want more bad news coming to you, do not be the one to start spreading it around to others. By giving others that which you desire, you indirectly increase that which comes back to you.

The Law of Action must be applied in order for us to manifest things on earth. We must engage in actions that support our words, feelings, vision, thoughts, dreams, and emotions. These actions will bring us manifestations of various results, which are dependent on our specifically chosen words, thoughts, dreams, and emotions.

The Law of Correspondence states that our outer world is a direct reflection of our inner world. "As above, so below. As within, so without." A good example of this law is the fact that in the physical world, energy, vibration, light, and motion have their corresponding principles in the Universe. This explains the relationship between the world of the infinite small and the infinite large, otherwise called microcosm and macrocosm, respectively.

The Law of Cause and Effect states that nothing happens by chance or outside the Universal Laws. We have to take responsibility for everything that happens in our lives. Every action has an equal reaction or consequence. "What we sow, that we reap." You cannot plant a hibiscus flower and expect to reap a rose. In other words every thought, action, and word is full of energy.

The Law of Compensation is the extended arm of the Law of Cause and Effect, which is applied to abundance and blessings that flow into our lives in the form of friendships, gifts, money, inheritances, and other forms of blessings. These various forms of compensation are the visible effects of our direct and indirect actions carried out throughout our lives.

The Law of Attraction shows how we create the events, people, and things that come into our lives. All our thoughts, words, feelings, and actions give out energies, which likewise attract like energies. Positive energies will always attract positive energies while negative energies will always attract negative energies. It doesn't matter whether you want the negative or not. What you put your attention on is what you attract into your life. On the other hand, if you do not like the negative, you just need to raise your vibration higher and away from it in order to fully apply the Law of Attraction to work for you. For example, when anyone starts out thinking negatively, his or her vibration is lowered. As the focus on the problem rather than the solution becomes intense, the size and number of the problem will magnify, as that is where the person's focus is.

The Law of Perpetual Transmutation of Energy states that we all have power within us to change any condition in our lives that we are not happy with. Higher energy vibrations will definitely consume and transform lower ones. Therefore we can change the energies in our lives by understanding the

Universal Laws and applying the principles in such a way as to effect positive changes in our lives.

The Law of Relativity states that each person will receive series of situations or problems for the purpose of strengthening the inner light within him or her. This law makes it possible for us to stay connected to our hearts when we proceed to solve problems or remedy situations, which are tests for us. This law also teaches us to compare our situations to other people's problems and put everything into its right perspective. No matter how bad we perceive our situations to be, there is always someone who is in a more difficult or worse situation, thereby making it all relative. Nobody is ever given a problem he or she will be unable to handle. We already have the ability to handle them. Do not spend your time looking for happiness from the outside, as it already lies within you.

The Law of Polarity states that everything is on a continuum and has an opposite. There has to be darkness so we might appreciate light. There is solid and liquid, and we can see and feel the difference. We have the ability to suppress and transform undesirable thoughts by focusing on the opposite thoughts, thereby bringing the desired positive change.

The Law of Rhythm states that everything vibrates and moves to a certain rhythm. This rhythm establishes cycles, seasons, patterns, and stages of development. Each cycle is a reflection of the regularity of God's universe. To master each rhythm, you must rise above any negative part of the cycle.

The Law of Gender states that everything has its masculine (yang) and feminine (yin) principles, and these are the basis for all creation in the Universe. As spiritual beings, we must ensure there is a balance between the masculine and feminine energies within us to overcome polarity and to realise our oneness.

3

GOOD VIBRATIONS

Everything in the Universe vibrates, moves, and travels in circular patterns. The same principle of vibration in the physical world apply to our feelings, desires, thoughts, dreams and will. Each sound, thought or thing has its own unique vibrational frequency. When you hear people say "like attracts like," they are actually referring to how a vibrational energy can resonate with or is attracted to the same or a similar vibrational energy.

WE ARE ENERGY, and we are surrounded by energy. Everything in the Universe is energy at its most basic level, and so are we. Within this sea of energy, each of us has our own unique energy field, our own unique energy pattern or vibration; we each have a unique song that resonates with the soul.

There is an energy field created by your thoughts, your emotions, your actions, your beliefs, and your experiences. It is created by the electrochemical processes occurring within your physical body all the time. Created by your very existence. This part of your energy field emanates from you and surrounds you and is often referred to as the aura.

The second component of your energy field is the universal life force energy flowing through and around you and your energy field. There are many layers, or bodies, within this energy field and many energy pathways as well. Each layer of your energy field is typically associated with an aspect of you—for example, the physical, mental, emotional, and spiritual bodies. There are also many pathways within this energy field along which energy flows, connecting the different layers or energy bodies to each other. Maintaining a state of balance in the body is called homeostasis. It is amazing how many of the body's systems are involved in maintaining balance: the right temperature, the right balance of electrolytes, the correct balance of hormones, and so on. In addition many systems are designed to prevent the build-up of wastes and toxins to help ensure the balance and healthy functioning of the body.

The human body is designed to be in a certain state of balance in order to function properly. And this state of balance is associated with the overall wellness or health of the individual. It is not something we have to think about or make happen; it is programmed into the body's very nature.

Problems may arise when the body's ability to maintain homeostasis is disrupted in some way. This disruption can be in the form of something that impacts the body directly from outside itself, like being involved in an accident or dropping something on your foot. It can also occur when an essential nutrient or something else that the body needs to function correctly is not provided. It can be more indirect—the stress of our lifestyles or our emotions can have negative impacts on our bodies, interfering with our bodies' ability to repair and maintain themselves.

A problem in one part of the body eventually has an impact on every other part of the body. The same concepts hold true on the mental, emotional, and spiritual levels in that balance is innate. It is when we are blocked in some way or are impacted by what is around us that we lose our balance.

Just as blood flows through your circulatory system, bringing nutrients to cells and removing harmful wastes, universal life force energy travels along the pathways of your energy systems. This life force energy not only nourishes and supports every cell of your body; it provides nourishment and support to you on the mental, emotional, and spiritual levels as well.

These aspects of your being are intimately connected to each other, and a problem in one can have an effect on the others. When the flow of life force energy within your energy field is disrupted, blocked, or out of balance, the healthy functioning of this energy field is impaired. This can manifest as mental, emotional, physical, or spiritual issues within your life.

The Law of Attraction shows how we create the events, people and things that come into our lives. All our thoughts, words, feelings and actions give out energies, which likewise attract like energies. Positive energies will always attract positive energies while negative energies will always attract negative energies. It doesn't matter whether you want the negative or not. What you place your attention on is what you attract into your life.

Our energies respond to and are affected by the energies around us and by our environment. They can also be affected by our experiences and our life circumstances. Most importantly they are affected by our responses to the outside influences in our lives. Every thought, every emotion we have has an energy to it that affects our energy field. Every belief we have has an energy pattern that affects our energy field. As toxins can build up in our bloodstream that can block the entire elimination system and eventually poison the body, so our energy fields can become a toxic wasteland if we hold on to emotions, thoughts, and energy patterns that are negative. Our energy fields are affected by what we do, think, hear, and say, as our environment affects it if we allow it to.

The fact that the human body is made of more than 70 percent water and earth is made up of about 80 percent water shows our thoughts can have profound implications on our health and the well being of the planet. Dr. Masaru Emoto, the Japanese scientist and water researcher, revealed the true nature of water and how thoughts, words, and vibrations affect the molecular structure of water.

He was a renowned researcher who gained worldwide acclaim by showing how water is deeply connected to our individual and collective consciousness. Born in Japan, he was a graduate of the Yokahama Municipal University's Department of Humanities and Sciences, with a focus on international relations. In 1992 he received certification from the Open International University as a doctor of alternative medicine. Dr Emoto is the author of

LIVING IN THE SPACE OF LIGHT

several best-selling books, including *The Hidden Messages in Water, The True Power of Water,* and *The Secret Life of Water.* He headed the worldwide Hado Instructor School, where he taught the ancient principle of hado, or life-force vibration.

Dr. Masaru Emoto revealed the effect of thoughts and words on the molecular structure of water. He discovered that water from clear springs and water that has been exposed to loving words show brilliant, complex, and colourful snowflake patterns while water from polluted sources or water exposed to negative thoughts forms incomplete, asymmetrical patterns with dull colours. Positive words, thoughts, and prayers create beautiful hexagonal water crystals, but negative ones will create formless, dark water crystals. Our thoughts and words have profound impacts on all living creatures and the earth.

Positive thoughts and words have the ability to make all related things beautiful and harmonised. Let your actions be based on the thoughts of love and gratitude. Love is a giving energy, and gratitude is a receiving energy. If you always have these two words in your mind and your actions are based on these concepts, you can naturally give people positive energy and bring harmony and balance to everything around you!

During an interview Dr. Emoto was asked about the holy river of Ganges in India, one of the most polluted rivers in the country, which has high levels of toxic pollutants. In spite of that, thousands of devotees bathe in the Ganges each day, with the belief that it prevents diseases. Do you think the positive thoughts of the devotees affect the holy Ganges to an extent that it prevents large-scale epidemics? Research has also stated that the Ganges has special self-purifying properties. Do you think the molecular structure of the river Ganges might be distorted yet have some healing vibration?

I think God created water with love as an active energy and gratitude as a passive energy. Water in River Ganges is sacred and it is god's water for Hindu people so the water contains lots of love and gratitude for them. Therefore, with these positive thoughts, water in River Ganges, which is physically polluted, can become holy water.

However, if foreign tourists drink that water, they would immediately get sick. I would also imagine if a pious Hindu learnt how to take water crystal photos, they would get the most beautiful looking water crystals from the water in River Ganges.

The fact that everything in nature is energy was known long before Albert Einstein articulated it. Ancient cultures also knew that everything is sound, oscillation, and rhythm, and that our bodies consist of colour and light. Physicists discovered some time ago that each individual cell gives off light and that it is possible to make this light visible. Further, it changes when the condition of the cell changes.

Many are extremely reluctant to accept that the body houses feelings, thoughts, and instincts that all play big roles where illness is concerned. Many do not realise thoughts and feelings also heal. We have all experienced this first hand. How do we feel when we are in love? We are ready to take on anything! Do you know anyone who became ill in the midst of falling in love? How do we feel when we are depressed, suffer from stress, or are desperate? What had cooled in your soul the last time you caught a cold? We know all the connections and do not need textbooks to verify them. They tell us only one thing: health is a matter of many various energies and connections.

Strange things happen in nature. They have all been proven scientifically and can be easily duplicated, but they cannot all be explained with modern methods.

When pests attack trees at the edge of a forest, the affected trees produce certain chemicals in self-defence. Not only that but simultaneously, the trees at the other end of the forest react the same way, even though the arrival of the pest is still a few weeks away.

When kittens are taken too early from the mother cat, they barely learn to catch mice, if at all. They remain amateur hunters for a long time. If you put these incapable kittens into a cage at night to sleep in the same room with caged cats that are experienced hunters (so the experienced cats cannot demonstrate their hunting skills), the young cats learn within a few days how to catch mice without ever having seen it.

LIVING IN THE SPACE OF LIGHT

A plant expert who took a long trip to Europe did an experiment. He wired the large leaves of his favourite houseplant to numerous instruments to measure electrical currents in the plant. While in Europe he kept a diary in which he made note of high-stress situations—when he was stuck in traffic, shortly before a big speech, a split second of fear, and so on. When he returned home after six weeks, he discovered the measuring devices on his plant had spiked during those moments when he was under great stress in Europe.

A nursing mother is visiting a neighbour miles away while her baby is peacefully sleeping at home. Suddenly, in the middle of the conversation, the mother starts lactating at the same time the baby wakes up hungry.

From the book *The Hundredth Monkey* by Ken Keyes Jr.)

In Japan Macaca fuscata monkeys were observed in the wild for a period of over thirty years.

In 1952, on the island of Koshima, scientists were providing monkeys with sweet potatoes dropped in the sand. The monkeys liked the taste of the raw sweet potatoes, but they found the dirt unpleasant.

An eighteen-month-old female named Imo found she could solve the problem by washing the potatoes in a nearby stream. She taught this trick to her mother. Her playmates also learned this new way, and they taught their mothers too. Various monkeys, before the eyes of the scientists, gradually picked up this cultural innovation.

Between 1952 and 1958, all the young monkeys learned to wash the sandy sweet potatoes to make them more palatable. Only the adults who imitated their children learned this social improvement. Other adults kept eating the dirty sweet potatoes.

Then something startling took place. In the autumn of 1958, a certain number of Koshima monkeys were washing sweet potatoes—the exact number is not known. Let us suppose that when the sun rose one morning, there were ninety-nine monkeys on Koshima Island who had learned to wash their sweet potatoes. Let's further suppose that later that morning, the hundredth monkey learned to wash potatoes.

— 21 —

Then it happened! By that evening almost everyone in the tribe was washing sweet potatoes before eating them. The added energy of this hundredth monkey somehow created an ideological breakthrough!

These scientists observed a most surprising thing: the habit of washing sweet potatoes then jumped over the sea. Colonies of monkeys on other islands and the mainland troop of monkeys at Takasakiyama began washing their sweet potatoes.

Thus, when a certain critical number achieves awareness, this new awareness may be communicated from mind to mind. Although the exact number may vary, this hundredth monkey phenomenon means that when only a limited number of people know of a new way, it may remain the conscious property of these people. But there is a point at which if only one more person tunes in to a new awareness, a field is strengthened so this awareness is picked up by almost everyone!

The question is how the information might have been transmitted. What is the common denominator? The answer is that we are beings of light—every living thing is. The electric processes of our bodies determine to the highest degree that we are beings of light as well as how our bodies work and how they communicate with our immediate environments, the world, and the Universe at large.

4

A TOUCH OF LOVE

We are spiritual beings on a path of loving service,
Where, if we pay attention to the sacred earth wisdom within—
Truth will direct our destinies to a place of peace where joy and
love abound.
Embrace how beautiful you are and you make your life a garden
of grace and beauty.
We are love and love is the light within that guides our way.

WHAT DOES IT mean to be a being of light and love? The ability to love is what activates the light within and around you. Every step you take, every move you make is important. It is an opportunity to light up the world! Your unique vibration brings change all around you. This is a very powerful statement. You are important to the world!

It is so good to know I am of value. It gives a sense of purpose. A sense of purpose triggers alertness and gets the ball rolling to do something. So what am I supposed to do? Let's go back…being of light and love. Your ability to love…

I must love more? "Love thy neighbour like thyself." That is going to be very difficult because how can I love someone who stole from me and tried to make a fool of me in front of my friends? And how can I forgive when I was cheated on? And how can I forget I was molested as a child? The list keeps on getting longer. And what about me? Why must I always be the least? I also have rights in this world, you know?

It is sometimes good to let the internal dialogue flow—not too often, though. Only if you are aware of what the grievances are can you let them go as easily as sweeping dust and dirt out of the kitchen door.

Love is the driving force of the Universe and behind all life in its journey back to the oneness of all things. Love is the almighty drive that sends people to the extremes of human endeavour. It provides the opportunity to learn and evolve.

There are many forms of love. There is the love of a mother for her child, the love of a child for parents, or the camaraderie of people of like mind. There is the love shown by self-sacrifice in order to save others during a crisis. There is love for nature and the whole range of colourful creations, animals, birds, trees, and plants. The list can go on and on till we get to the realisation that love can be found anywhere and everywhere.

Love is light. It enlightens those who give and receive it. Love is gravity because it makes some people feel attracted to others. Love is power because it multiplies the best we have and allows humanity not to be extinguished in their blind selfishness. Love unfolds and reveals. For love we live and die. Love is God, and God is love. There is only love, the one energy that pervades all existence upon all frequencies of consciousness.

There are chemical processes in the brain that affect how we feel. When we're with a loved one, the body releases hormones, like oxytocin and dopamine, that signal feelings of trust, pleasure, and reward. At the centre of how our bodies respond to love and affection is a hormone called oxytocin. Most of our oxytocin is made in the area of the brain called the hypothalamus. Some is released into our bloodstream, but much of its effect is thought to reside in the brain. Oxytocin makes us feel good when we're close to family and other loved ones, including pets. It does this by acting through what scientists call the dopamine reward system. Dopamine is a brain chemical that plays a crucial part in how we perceive pleasure. Oxytocin does more than make us feel good. It lowers the levels of stress hormones in the body, reducing blood pressure, improving mood, increasing tolerance for pain and

LIVING IN THE SPACE OF LIGHT

perhaps even speeding how fast wounds heal. It also seems to play an important role in our relationships. It's been linked, for example, to how much we trust others.

Love activates areas in the brain that are responsible for motivation, emotion, attention, and memory. It has the ability to influence stress reduction and pain relief and has consequences for an overall sense of well being as well as mental and physical health. The happiness and euphoria triggered by the hormones and chemicals the brain produces in response to being in love can stimulate productivity and have positive effects on experiencing pleasurable and deeply rewarding experiences.

While feeling loved appears to benefit our heart's health, giving love seems to do the same for our ageing process. The results of a study of more than seven hundred elderly adults showed that the effects of ageing were influenced more by what the participants contributed to their social support networks than what they received from them. In other words the more love and support they gave, the more they benefited. In the end it will not matter how much money you made or how well you did on that work project but how well you loved in this world.

Make a conscious choice to open your heart to love. Decide today that sharing love will be a priority for you. Share appreciation for someone. Appreciate a quality someone has—his or her kindness, compassion, integrity, or creativity.

Let go of past hurts and open up to love. The reality of the open heart is that you will hurt sometimes when your heart is open, but that is OK. You will survive.

Surrender is the easiest act for the soul and the hardest act for the ego. Surrender breaks you down and reorganises every part of you when you sincerely ask for love to enter your life and for you to live this life beckoned by the call of the soul that desires to recognise itself. Surrender makes us gentle, soft, and transparent. In surrender, all the things you have to fight for or against are conquered, and a new way of living arises.

The journey through our aspects—me, myself, and I—is our greatest life challenge. Acceptance is part of self-love on a much more profound level.

— 25 —

With acceptance we acknowledge our humanity and all of its foibles and invite our divinity to share our table even though we're eating on paper plates, using paper towels as napkins, and using plastic cutlery. Our divinity doesn't need the special china and silver; it just needs an invitation to sit next to us.

We look at ourselves very critically because we can't get over the pain, shame, and guilt of the past to see how we can ever become the containers for the joy, peace, love, and fulfilment that we long for. So we see ourselves as incomplete and broken and set out on endless paths of healing that try to make sense of pasts we can't resolve and create presents we can't envision.

Our "myself" aspect is the starting point for our new being-ness. It is the self we criticise, judge, hate, blame, shame, guilt, and despise for its pain, weakness, and fears. When we focus on our "myself" aspect, we see everything we believe is the source of our pain, our mistakes, and our lack of progress or success.

In the "myself" aspect is the seed for the I because we achieve congruence through acceptance of who we have been, not by rejecting it. Once we can accept ourselves fully and completely, we open the portal to allow our divinity to shine through. Divinity is about wholeness, not holiness. It does not arrive on our doorstep when we are good enough; it arrives when we acknowledge that nothing about us is imperfect or irredeemable. Our fear state exists because we reject the blessings of our divinity and when we think we are not good enough to be divine. This is the "I" aspect, the part of us that holds the key to the joy, love, peace, and fulfilment we desire. This is also our recognition of ourselves as a part of God and that nothing we ever do can separate us from this aspect. We arrive at our "I" aspect when we are ready to accept ourselves, warts and all, and acknowledge our own perfection.

Beauty is about you—be-*you*-tiful. Not others and their definitions. Don't wait for someone else to tell you that you are loveable, worthy, or beautiful. Tell yourself. Loving who you are is the most empowering thing you will ever do for yourself, your life here, and those around you.

Many of us were brought up in times when it was thought to be the least to be humble. Kids were supposed to be seen, not heard. We were told, "Stop being a naughty child and go to sleep now." Shame was used to curtail behaviour through negative thoughts and feelings about ourselves. We were not raised with the imprints of awesomeness on every level. Some of us were lucky to be more beautiful or clever than others or to excel in sports. Those lucky ones could work from the snippets of memory to be valued at some stage of life. Most of humanity suffers from a lack of self-love, from a lack of knowing you are awesome and loved and feeling safe in your own skin, regardless of what you look like or what your mental or physical abilities are.

But I grew up like that. How can I now learn to love myself more?

It is a process of going within your body and mind. Spend time with you. Give yourself the loving, nurturing care you deserve. Give yourself at least five minutes a day to be alone with you. Do not share this time with anyone. If you develop a small ritual with the intention to dwell in your own sacred space, it will become more powerful every time you do it.

Create a personal affirmation to remind you of your true value, beauty, and worth. You may use a single word or a simple sentence. Choose something that feels good, strong, and powerful for you. You can write it on a note and put it in your pocket or purse, stick it were you can see it, paint it, or just memorise and repeat it whenever you need a little boost throughout your day.

When you say your affirmation, try to really feel the truth of the statement in your body.

"I am magnificent."

"I am beautiful, inside and out."

"I see and feel my true beauty."

"I walk with beauty before me and all around me."

"I am thankful for all I am and all I can be."

Self-love is not how you feel about yourself. It's what you do for yourself. You can love yourself only by doing, not thinking.

How can we be the very best we can be if we don't love ourselves? Over the years I've come to recognise the importance of self-love and have slowly begun to integrate practices that help me love myself a little bit more each day. Give yourself a pat on the back for all your little accomplishments; you deserve it!

Stop judging your present self or comparing it to your past self.

Forgive yourself for things you have done in the past; you did the best you could at the time.

Learn about how to treat your body well, and give it only the best.

Listen to your body, and honour its subtle requests—that is, hunger, satiety, fatigue, and sickness.

Keep moving the body, and never stop.

Be creative in your thoughts and actions.

Read things that spark your creativity or inspire you.

Treat yourself to at-home spa treatments and nurture your body with aromatherapy oils and baths, light candles and listen to beautiful music.

Stop worrying about things that haven't happened and may never happen.

Declutter your surroundings.

Surround yourself with positive people, and let them help you along the way.

Take five minutes of quiet time each day to just float in the stillness.

Stop feeling sorry for yourself, and stop playing the victim. You're giving your power away.

Practise positive affirmations in front of the mirror daily.

There is nothing on this earth you will ever do that does not require the cooperation of your body. Be grateful for each cell in your body. Be nice to it. Don't poison it, don't abuse it, and don't neglect it. Disrespect towards your body will undermine any attempt to love yourself. Love it with your actions, or it won't love you back. If you are rude to it, it will hinder you, embarrass you, and even kill you.

Cultivate respect. The quality of your actions matters. Do everything with care. Pick up and put down objects as if you respect them. Don't just drop yourself into a seat; sit down with purpose. Respect everything you buy, borrow, give away, or dispose of. Respect your time. Spend your time on things that put you into a better situation in life, on things that make you more capable, rather than on things that make you feel good for the moment. You will love yourself for doing this.

Respect the world around you. The spectacles, the scenes, the details. Respect buildings and the people who built them. Respect businesses and the people who run them. Respect the trees. Respect the tiny yellow-flowered

LIVING IN THE SPACE OF LIGHT

weed that vehemently persists in thrusting itself up through the crack in the sidewalk. It invests all its energy in growing, and it absolutely insists on being itself.

Respect other people. Respect their skills, their virtues, and their flaws. Respect their thoughts. Let them finish what they are saying; don't interrupt; don't be dismissive. Try to understand what they're getting at. Let them be who they are. People are exactly as judgmental about themselves as they are about others. Find the value in others, or you will never see it in yourself. Forget the ways in which you would like other people to be different. Forgive them, and forgive yourself. Forgive yourself every time you wake up and every time you go to bed. Forgive yourself every time you do something wrong.

Forgiveness is the greatest gift you can give yourself because it sets you free from energetic bonds and attachments that can suck the life force out of you. The energy of an eye for an eye keeps the vibration of a person very low. All good comes from forgiveness. It is a truth that the continuation of the human species is due to being forgiving. Forgiveness is holiness. By forgiveness the Universe is held together. Forgiveness is the might of the mighty; forgiveness is quiet of mind.

Each life is an assuming of ancient obligations, a recovery of old relations, an opportunity for the paying of old indebtedness, a chance to make restitution and progress, an awakening of deep-seated qualities, a recognition of old friends and enemies, the solution of revolting injustices, and the explanation of that which conditions the man and makes him what he is.

The first person you probably have not forgiven is yourself. More people have a lack of forgiveness towards themselves than towards anybody else. People must forgive all who need forgiveness. If the first person to forgive is yourself, you need to say, "God, before you, I forgive myself. Whatever I have done, I accept your forgiveness, and I forgive me." That's a very simple but profound statement because as long as we feel we are under condemnation, we will never have faith to see miracles.

Secondly we have to forgive God Himself if we have bitterness. There are people who blame God because a child died, because a husband ran away, because they have been sick, because they have not had enough money. Consciously or unconsciously they think all of these things are God's fault. There is deep-seated resentment; yet you cannot be resentful towards God and experience miracles. You have to rid yourself of any bitterness towards God. That may take some soul searching. You must ask yourself, "Am I blaming God for my situation?"

The problem for many of us is that sometimes we can choose to forgive another, but still, in our heart of hearts, the anger or resentment lingers. However, it is in fact possible to forgive and truly let go of past disappointments, hurts, or blatant acts of abuse. Although at times this may seem implausible, forgiveness is a teachable and learnable skill that can dramatically improve with practice over time.

The best way to give up a grudge and forgive someone who has hurt, disappointed, or betrayed you is to change the way you develop your grievance story. This is the story you tell yourself (and possibly others) over and over about the way you were maltreated and the way you became the victimised. Learn to cast your story in such a way that you become a survivor of difficult times or, better yet, the hero of your story. As you continue to reshape your grievance story—becoming the hero of that story, developing empathy and compassion for the abuser, and celebrating your strengths—you will undoubtedly begin to notice a shift in your consciousness. Your feelings of anger and sadness are likely to quiet down, and your self-esteem is likely to blossom, as will your relationships.

Forgiveness is one of the eight positive emotions that keep us connected with our deepest selves and with others. These positive emotions are key ingredients that bind us together in our humanity. They are love, forgiveness, hope, joy, compassion, faith, awe, and gratitude.

Joe Vitale recalls his introduction to an ancient Hawaiian healing process:

Two years ago, I heard about a therapist in Hawaii who cured a complete ward of criminally insane patients—without ever seeing any of them. The psychologist would study an inmate's chart and then

LIVING IN THE SPACE OF LIGHT

look within himself to see how he created that person's illness. As he improved himself, the patient improved.

When I first heard this story, I thought it was an urban legend. How could anyone heal anyone else by healing himself? How could even the best self-improvement master cure the criminally insane? It didn't make any sense. It wasn't logical, so I dismissed the story.

However, I heard it again a year later. I heard that the therapist had used a Hawaiian healing process called ho'oponopono. I had never heard of it, yet I couldn't let it leave my mind. If the story was at all true, I had to know more. I had always understood "total responsibility" to mean that I am responsible for what I think and do. Beyond that, it's out of my hands. I think that most people think of total responsibility that way. We're responsible for what we do, not what anyone else does—but that's wrong.

The Hawaiian therapist who healed those mentally ill people would teach me an advanced new perspective about total responsibility. His name is Dr. Ihaleakala Hew Len. We probably spent an hour talking on our first phone call. I asked him to tell me the complete story of his work as a therapist. He explained that he worked at Hawaii State Hospital for four years. That ward where they kept the criminally insane was dangerous.

Psychologists quit on a monthly basis. The staff called in sick a lot or simply quit. People would walk through that ward with their backs against the wall, afraid of being attacked by patients. It was not a pleasant place to live, work, or visit.

Dr. Len told me that he never saw patients. He agreed to have an office and to review their files. While he looked at those files, he would work on himself. As he worked on himself, patients began to heal.

"After a few months, patients that had to be shackled were being allowed to walk freely," he told me. "Others who had to be heavily medicated were getting off their medications. And those who had no

— 31 —

chance of ever being released were being freed." I was in awe. "Not only that," he went on, "but the staff began to enjoy coming to work. Absenteeism and turnover disappeared. We ended up with more staff than we needed because patients were being released, and all the staff was showing up to work. Today, that ward is closed."

This is where I had to ask the million dollar question: "What were you doing within yourself that caused those people to change?"

"I was simply healing the part of me that created them," he said. I didn't understand. Dr. Len explained that total responsibility for your life means that everything in your life—simply because it is in your life—is your responsibility. In a literal sense the entire world is your creation.

Whew. This is tough to swallow. Being responsible for what I say or do is one thing. Being responsible for what everyone in my life says or does is quite another. Yet, the truth is this: if you take complete responsibility for your life, then everything you see, hear, taste, touch, or in any way experience is your responsibility because it is in your life. This means that terrorist activity, the president, the economy or anything you experience and don't like—is up for you to heal. They don't exist, in a manner of speaking, except as projections from inside you. The problem isn't with them, it's with you, and to change them, you have to change you.

I know this is tough to grasp, let alone accept or actually live. Blame is far easier than total responsibility, but as I spoke with Dr. Len, I began to realize that healing for him and in ho'oponopono means loving yourself.

If you want to improve your life, you have to heal your life. If you want to cure anyone, even a mentally ill criminal you do it by healing you.

I asked Dr. Len how he went about healing himself. What was he doing, exactly, when he looked at those patients' files?

"I just kept saying, 'I'm sorry' and 'I love you' over and over again," he explained.

LIVING IN THE SPACE OF LIGHT

That's it?

That's it.

Turns out that loving yourself is the greatest way to improve yourself, and as you improve yourself, you improve your world.

Let me give you a quick example of how this works: one day, someone sent me an email that upset me. In the past I would have handled it by working on my emotional hot buttons or by trying to reason with the person who sent the nasty message.

This time, I decided to try Dr. Len's method. I kept silently saying, "I'm sorry" and "I love you," I didn't say it to anyone in particular. I was simply evoking the spirit of love to heal within me what was creating the outer circumstance.

Within an hour I got an e-mail from the same person. He apologized for his previous message. Keep in mind that I didn't take any outward action to get that apology. I didn't even write him back. Yet, by saying "I love you," I somehow healed within me what was creating him.

Suffice it to say that whenever you want to improve anything in your life, there's only one place to look: inside you. When you look, do it with love.

Ho'oponopono is not a religion and never will become one. There are no teachers, gurus or high priests or middlemen. Practitioners know that the Creator is the only teacher there is. Indeed, there are those who are more experienced in the practice of Ho'oponopono, but they are regarded in the same way you would regard an older brother or sister.

Ho'oponopono is a tool for atonement, for correcting errors, erasing the effects of past actions and memories that cause havoc and grief in our lives, the lives of others and on Mother Nature as a whole.

There is a choice in every moment, between acting out of love or out of fear. At any instant you can stop and look at the moment, and it will be clear which action is love and which is fear. Make a habit out of choosing one or the other.

CAARNA

You won't be able to have respect if you do not make a habit of recognising value. There is value in every person, object, place, and moment, but you may miss it if you hold faults to be more important. Find the endless value in the world around you, and it will be easy to find the endless value in yourself. Eventually you will no longer see a difference between the two.

5

Every Moment Counts

THE ONLY MOMENT we have is now. This is where we create. What we have done is done, and that moment in history exists only as a record or energy trace in time and space. The consequences of past actions are atoned for through karma and can be rewritten to a degree. The future only ever happens in and from the present tense and is built of today's thoughts, dressed by emotion, and driven by action. Activity is the key.

While there is nothing wrong with being a "creature of habit," it is your habits that either enliven you or slowly withdraw life force energy from you. Life is meant to be lived openly, as an adventure and an exploration of self. Life is a never-ending series of present moments in which you get to choose your experience, based on your God given guidance and soul-level desires. Your desires inspired you to grow. Your guidance tries to help you grow gracefully and kindly.

Perhaps you have a desire to try something new—a class, a food, a career, or a hobby. Your heart feels excited. Your mind starts to offer all sorts of reasons why you should ignore the heart, "You're too old. You don't have enough time. You read an article on the Internet that says this isn't good for you. What makes you think you could do that?" Your mind makes excuses and you give up before you even give your heart a chance.

Maybe you would not have liked the new food, but you would have learned something useful from someone in the grocery store or restaurant.

— 35 —

Maybe you wouldn't have maintained the hobby, but you'd meet a dear friend along the way. Maybe you're guided into a new career and then fired, only to discover this is a stepping-stone to your dream job. If you don't listen to the heart, you may never discover its reasons. If you don't remain open to life and your instincts in each moment, you might miss the fullest life you could be living.

Use your mind to review the past, but always pay attention as well to how you feel right here, right now. While the mind may argue against the heart, the heart always knows the kindest and most loving path…in each moment.

Change breathes fresh air into our minds, hearts, homes, bodies, souls, and lives. But it isn't always easy. I may want new thoughts but giving up my old ones requires some willpower and dedication. I may want to try new foods but that meant I have to branch out a bit and risk a little failure here and there.

Change requires letting go. Pay attention to your loving desires, when you feel a desire in the moment to do something, say something loving, or try something that appeals and feels wholesome (because your guidance is always loving), say it, do it, try it. Pick up the phone and call that person you are thinking about. Write the email. Sign up for a class. Get outside and take a walk. Take a ten-minute nap. Look at that new career online. Go up to that stranger and compliment them! Get the food that sounds appealing and healthy. Politely bow out of a conversation that is annoying or boring you. When you feel something that sounds loving, wholesome, appealing…say it, do it, try it. Trust. The heart has its reasons.

Use Your Mind, but don't let it Rule You. Sometimes we're disconnected from our hearts. We've ignored them for so long we can't hear our true desires. Instead you hear secondary desires that don't really satisfy. For example, say you've ignored your desire to eat food that nurtures you for so long that you are now low on energy. Now your body wants sugar, carbs, and things your mind already knows from past experience don't feel so good. Thank the mind for reminding you. Now sit quietly and ask your heart…Heart what does my body really want right now? You'll get the answer.

Your mind is a useful tool for analysing current situations against knowledge, past experience, and desired outcomes. Used correctly, it can inform

LIVING IN THE SPACE OF LIGHT

you and let you know whether or not something is in alignment with your heart.

Every now and then have a little "heart time." In this age of so much information, we all need a little time to get back in touch with our hearts. We know when we're disconnected. We feel stressed, tired, angry, upset, ill, and so on. At these times it is important to spend some quiet time alone. Journal, ponder, walk in nature, listen to beautiful music. Ask your heart, "What do you need? Am I listening? Am I ignoring you? Given my desires, what next?"

To be in the moment requires your full attention on what you are busy with. Be focused to make the most of each moment. If you are busy making a cup of coffee, pour your heart and soul into it. Watch the process of pouring steaming-hot water over the coffee, add a bit of love, smell the aroma of the coffee, and feel your mouth salivating. Engage as many of your senses as possible in the moment. It forms lasting memories that can be treasured for the rest of your life.

I still remember the smell of my grade one classroom at break time, when we all sat at our desks and opened our lunch boxes that were packed with so much love and care. I remember the sound of wax paper crinkling as we opened our sandwiches with much expectation. What did Mom put on the bread today? And that smell of fresh bread that filled the classroom. The first bite of the teeth through the bread and the lingering of that bite on the tongue before the explosion of good, wholesome taste filled my being.

To be in the moment is to make the most of each moment to leave a lasting, precious memory for all who take part in it. Multitasking is something that mothers know how to do, but be careful of letting the opportunity slip through your fingers to make the moment a golden one. Become invested in what you do; be mindful of the process; set an intention of the outcome you want to see. If you are packing lunch boxes for the family, do it with love, and add a small detail as a token of your love. They may not say anything, but they will experience the vibration of love you put into it.

My mother raised six children, and to this day I remember her small tokens of love—the thin, delicate sandwiches cut in triangles because I liked them like that. Always neatly wrapped in wax paper because I liked to unwrap them. A lunch table laid with a floral tablecloth and matching china especially for her children when they came home from school. A glass of milk and a cookie if you studied late at night. She remembered how each one of us liked things to be done and showed us she was mindful of that when she performed her endless tasks as mother of six.

Words and thoughts are vibrations that can affect us in positive or negative ways. Positive means of a higher vibration, which is what we strive to be and do to improve who we are. Our words and thoughts create the reality we live in. High-vibration thoughts of love, compassion, kindness, and beauty will attract those into our reality.

Choose to raise your vibration moment by moment. It takes awareness of what you are thinking, doing, planning every moment. It requires being focused on adding a touch of love to everything you think about and do. Living in the moment means being absorbed by what is in front of you now. Move the past and the future out of the way, and do not allow any thoughts that are not of the moment to enter your mind.

Clear your mind of negative patterns of thought. Learn to control the chattering mind that goes around in circles all day long and that has the ability to drive you totally crazy. Remember you can never leave empty space in the mind. If you clear negative patterns, you have to replace them with positive, uplifting patterns of thought. Otherwise the mind will quickly fill the space with more chattering. If a negative thought enters the mind, simply stop the thought and replace it with a happy memory or a happy song. Soon the mind will automatically skip to the happy song when the negative thought enters your mind. Mantras or affirmations can also be used to establish positive thought patterns.

Be grateful for life. For all you are and all you are not. For the good and the bad. For the expected and unexpected. For all you can see and the unseen. For being happy or sad, for loving or hating. Say thank you for all. Sit back and watch how gratitude transforms your life.

Be with yourself alone, and focus on your breath. Feel the movement of air from your nose to the lungs, and feel it filling your lungs. Feel the pressure rising until you release it. Feel the chest pushing the air out through

LIVING IN THE SPACE OF LIGHT

your mouth. Become part of the process: in…hold…out; in…hold…out. There will still be thoughts going through your mind. Don't mind them; just stay focused on your breath and what is happening in your body while you are breathing. Start doing this exercise on your own until it becomes a process that can be triggered by thinking of it. Eventually you will be able to do it anywhere, even in the midst of a rock concert or with chaos all around.

This exercise helps to gather yourself to your centre—it puts all your pieces together to enable you to act from a centred and grounded state, where there is stillness. If you can create stillness within yourself, everything around you seems to become calmer and more controlled. It allows you a firm basis from where to take action. Taking action from a solid platform gives stability and strength, which is needed when you take charge.

No longer do you need to feel like life is trying to pull you apart. When you take charge and believe you can deal with anything life throws at you, everything around you changes. It takes the decision to go within, and it takes persistence to explore. It takes being in the moment to find your stable platform where you will find strength to act and take control. Lastly it takes courage to have strong faith to know all will be well in the end.

Act lovingly towards yourself, and do things that nurture you, make you stronger, and make you proud of who you are and how you live your life. Exercise, meditate, help others freely, and eat a healthy diet. Practise progress, not perfection.

If you know how to love yourself, you will know how to love others. Start focusing on the positive things about your life that you really love. Stop complaining. See the glass as half full, or celebrate the empty space it leaves to be filled again. Be of service in the world. Nothing will help you find compassion within yourself and for others like coming face to face with people who have much less materially and way bigger problems than you.

Pay attention to the company you keep. Are you always around complainers and negative people? If so, you need to realise their energy can have a very negative effect on you. View relationships as opportunities to learn how to love unconditionally. When you are feeling challenged in a relationship, it is

— 39 —

an opportunity to learn to unconditionally love yourself and the other person more.

Accept that life is always changing. Do not resist change. Go with the flow.

Start appreciating the small things. Have you ever taken a close look at nature? The sky, animals, plants, rivers. It's absolutely gorgeous! Start seeking out and learning to appreciate life itself. Remember you shouldn't let life pass you by. You don't want to look at your life years from now and be unhappy you spent your time complaining and being negative. Do it now, while you have the chance.

> *When the heart opens, we forget ourselves and the world pours in: this world, and also the invisible world of meaning that sustains everything that was and ever shall be.*

—ROGER HOUSDEN, *TEN POEMS TO OPEN YOUR HEART*

6

GRATITUDE

MY GRATITUDE FOR life has been my driving force from a very early age, but I learned only later in life that it is also one of the most powerful tools we have to unlock the fullness life has in store for us.

At the age of twenty-one, I was handed a small book by one of my patients about gratitude. It recorded the series of changes a preacher experienced when he started to practise gratitude in daily life. I remember when I read the book, it felt totally out of place for the times we were living in then, which was the early '80s. Looking back at it now, it felt like I was travelling through time when I read it. The content was simple but profound. I had never come across information like that before, but it became my truth immediately as I read it, probably because I was already living like that in my space of light, without realising it.

Gratitude became my consciousness first and then my intention. I strived to live in a state of thankfulness from then on, and the Universe reacted by opening up a life filled with miracles to make me feel even more grateful.

Gratitude is more than saying thank you. It's a sense of wonder, appreciation and, yes, thankfulness for life. It's easy to go through life without recognising your good fortune. Often, it takes a serious illness or other tragic event to jolt people into appreciating the good things in their lives. Don't wait for something like that to happen to you. Make a commitment to practice gratitude. Each day identify at least one thing that enriches your life. Let gratitude

— 41 —

be the last thought before you go to sleep. Let gratitude also be your first thought when you wake up in the morning.

Gratitude is the most powerful emotion we can have. From an early age, we are taught to say thank you. This is one way of showing gratitude, but do we really mean it? Do we teach our children to feel the emotion of gratitude, or does it just become a habit without thought?

Yes, we should say thank you and feel the emotion or vibration radiate from the bottom of the heart, spreading through the body until it lights up the soul and shines on everything around us. Gratitude raises the vibration of our inner light and entire being. It's when we put feeling into our "thank you!" that it becomes valuable and life changing. It becomes valuable if we say it when we don't have to or when it is not expected of us.

When we are grateful, it increases our presence in the world.

"Gratitude is the magic key that unlocks the fullness of life. It turns what we have into enough, and more. It turns denial into acceptance, chaos into order and confusion into clarity. It turns problems into gifts, failures into success, the unexpected into perfect timing and mistakes into important events. Gratitude makes sense of our past, brings peace for today and creates a vision for tomorrow."

—MELODY BEATTIE

Gratitude sweetens our disposition, brightens our day, and encourages those around us. Gratitude will help make us healthy and is the antidote for every negative emotion in our lives. Anger, worry, fear, hostility, and doubt—all can be transformed by the practice of gratitude. You do not have to be happy to be grateful. Think about how you feel attracted to a positive person with passion—it draws friends and customers alike. Be grateful for all that is, for in it lies the power to create the miracles you wish to see in your life.

Say thank you for the challenges. No matter if the toast is burnt and the coffee cold—be grateful.

LIVING IN THE SPACE OF LIGHT

Say thank you for the challenges in your life because they give you opportunities to be stronger.

Say thank you for what makes you sad because it helps to lift the pain.

Say thank you where and when you find no love because it opens the heart to feel.

Say thank you for your loss because it opens the eyes to see that nothing is ever lost without being replaced with more blessing.

If the pain is too great or the burden too heavy, say thank you, even if you do not understand why. Soon you will experience the power of *gratitude*.

Living in a state of gratitude takes practise. View life as it presents itself to you, without a feeling of dread or judgment, of being dark or wrong or any of the negative labels we so love to attach to circumstances when things don't work out our way. It is what it is, and I am grateful for the opportunity to experience life. I ask myself how I can make this a memorable and worthy experience in my life.

Say thank you for everything whether you like it or not. Gratitude for emotional pain or grief makes it easier to bear. Say thank you over and over and over again until you feel the release of tension in your body and the heaviness lifting. Don't forget to say thank you for that too!

It is a good tool to let down steam or to control anger and frustration. Say thank you for the anger, and be passionate about it—it can have the same effect as punching a pillow or breaking something and is far less destructive.

7

THE BALANCING ACT

WHEN WE FOLLOW our hearts' desires and wisdom, we are naturally seeking balance and become more in touch with the environment, our lives, and ourselves overall. The heart understands this, but the mind cannot fully grasp it because the mind is so conditioned to a linear cause-and-effect mode of thinking. Yet the heart feels the truth and what is right at the time. Everything is one continuum that affects everything else.

There is no division between the physical, emotional, and mental aspects of our life events, all of which reflect the balance or imbalance of our energies. Therefore it is believed that the more we stray from living in harmony with the central point of balance or God and the spiritual laws of the Universe, the more certain it is that no form of external medicine or treatment could make up for the stresses that will affect the mind, body, and spirit.

It is not an intellectual exercise but more experiential. We learn as we go—and we learn as we eat, drink, think, and feel—along the lines of following seasonal changes and living in harmony with the elements. We acknowledge our emotions and move through them rather than avoid them.

There is a healing quality to nature, which has been known for centuries be it taking time to smell the roses, meditating on a mountain, lying in a wildflower field, strolling by a meandering stream or hiking in a forest. Hippocrates, the father of modern medicine, recognized this powerful attribute in his humbling statement:

LIVING IN THE SPACE OF LIGHT

"Nature cures—not the physician."

Our modern hermetically sealed lifestyle is turning many into indoor zombies with dulled senses, suppressed immune systems, depressed spirits and sharply increased risk for illness and disease. One can hardly call that living—particularly when the healing power of nature is so close at hand and literally, outside your front door. If you are suffering from a nature deficiency, the good news is that it's an easy fix—with benefits that have the power to change the course and quality of your life.

Symptoms come about when the self-regulating capacity of the body is overburdened. Such things as toxicity, stress, inefficient elimination, negative thoughts and emotions, inherited patterns, poor diet and nutritional deficiency may overburden the body. Symptoms are telling us that we need to look at what we are doing to our bodies and in our lives. The body has the ability to heal. There is wisdom inherent in nature that guides this process of healing.

Spending more time in Nature has many benefits, research studies show that medical patients heal faster, experience less pain and are more pleasant when their hospital experience includes views or sounds from nature both natural and artificially induced.

Several studies have demonstrated that time in nature contributes to emotional wellbeing. For example, people report they feel more relaxed and their blood pressure levels drop after being outdoors. Adults and teens both report increased self-esteem and are more cooperative and kind, with a positive outlook and view of other people, more self-confidence and patience.

Spending time in nature has positive impacts on those dealing with more serious issues such as depression, anxiety and ADHD. Participants in a study in England reported declines in their levels of depression when they spent time walking outside. Interestingly, they reported little benefit and occasional worsening of their symptoms when they did the same amount of walking in shopping malls.

Research also shows that being in nature can help those with concentration problems such as ADHD. Office workers pay more attention to detail if

— 45 —

they have a window. Time in nature enhances our ability to focus and perform better academically.

Some propose that continued focus on tasks leads to "direct attention fatigue" which can drain and debilitate us, leading to impulsivity, distractibility and irritability. The restorative effects found in nature can combat this.

Sunshine in moderation is essential to our health. It enables the body to create Vitamin D, which is key to boosting immunity and warding off serious disease. How to slip in a bit of sun without booking a flight to the Bahamas? Eat lunch outdoors a few times a week, point your face to the sun and get your dose of Vit D.

Stale office air, office carpets and chemical-spewing copy machines at work, all chip away at our overall health. Get out at lunchtime, even if it's just to pick up some food from down the street. While you're walking, take a few deep breaths and fill your lungs with fresh air instead of the re-circulated indoor stuff. It will help clear your lungs, boost alertness and reduce your exposure to office toxins.

Getting into the great outdoors doesn't necessarily mean climbing Kilimanjaro. Ten minutes on a park bench or your garden will help calm your mind and reconnect you with the natural world.

Listen to the world around you. Just as honking horns, barking dogs and crying babies can escalate irritation and blood pressure levels, soothing sounds from the natural world can calm the mind and body, and help bring blood pressure back down into the healthier range. Head outside, take the headphones off and listen to the sounds around you.

Make your brain work a little harder by exposing your eyes to the ever-changing light and colours of the natural world. More vivid than any computer screen, the colours found in nature actually force your brain to work a bit harder to process it all.

Explore new ground. Hug a tree. Lie in the grass. Dig your toes deep into the sand by the sea. Connect physically with the earth and natural world to energize your body. By making regular contact with the ground, you'll restore and help maintain the body's natural electrical balance, thereby promoting your optimal health.

True health just doesn't come in pill form—it comes from the things we do to promote our wellbeing.

> *The best remedy for those who are afraid, lonely or unhappy is to go outside, somewhere where they can be quite alone with the heavens, nature and God. Because only then does one appreciate the beauty of nature. As longs as this exists, and it certainly always will, I know that then there will always be comfort for every sorrow, whatever the circumstances may be. And I firmly believe that nature brings solace in all troubles.*

—ANNE FRANK, *THE DIARY OF A YOUNG GIRL*

The ancients believed that the experience of sacred geometry was essential to the education of the soul. They knew that these patterns and codes were symbolic of our own inner realm and the subtle structure of awareness. To them the "sacred" had particular significance involving consciousness and the profound mystery of awareness…the ultimate sacred wonder.

Clear examples of sacred geometry in nature and matter are seen in all types of crystals, natural and cultured; the hexagonal geometry of snowflakes; creatures exhibiting logarithmic spiral patterns—for example, snails and various shellfish; birds and flying insects exhibiting clear golden mean proportions in bodies and wings; the way in which lightning forms branches; the way in which rivers branch; the geometric molecular and atomic patterns that all solid metals exhibit; and the way in which a tree spans out so all its branches receive sunlight.

In space, nature's letters of creation are shapes; in time, they are rhythms. These rhythms range from the circadian rhythms that govern human life activity to the great cycles of time discussed and observed by major traditions around the world.

Sacred geometry takes on whole other level of significance when grounded in the experience of self-awareness. From the farthest reaches of the cosmos to the atomic structure of a single cell within the body, the same laws of form and mathematics apply. The secret to life is in these forms and numbers.

Most classical traditions see the forces of nature as being conscious, which means we have the potential to directly communicate with them. The laws of nature then become the expression of a consciousness inherent in our world. The abilities of shamans of native traditions to control and affect natural forces, such as weather patterns, observed and recorded for decades by anthropologists and other observers, become understandable when seen from this perspective.

Earth's magnetic field shields us from deadly cosmic radiation, and without it life, as we know it could not exist here. The motion of liquid iron in the planet's outer core, a phenomenon called a "geodynamo," generates the field. But how it was first created and then sustained throughout Earth's history has remained a mystery to scientists. New work published in *Nature* from a team led by Carnegie's Alexander Goncharov sheds light on the history of this incredibly important geologic occurrence.

The Planetary Energetic Grid Theory falls under the heading of pseudoscience. It operates through geometric patterns called Sacred Geometry. Lines meet at various intersecting points forming a grid or matrix. This is equivalent to the acupressure points on our bodies. These grid points can be found at some of the strongest power places on the planet.

Plato recognised grids and their patterns, devising a theory that the Earth's basic structure evolved from simple geometric shapes to more complex ones. These shapes became known as platonic solids: cube (4), tetrahedron (3), octahedron (8), dodecahedron (12), icosahedron (20). In *Timeaus*, Plato associated each shape with one of the elements: earth, fire, air, ether, and water.

The Earth's energy grids, from the beginnings of its evolutionary course, have evolved through each of these shapes to what it is today. Each shape, superimposed, one upon the other to create a kind of all encompassing energy field that is the very basis of Earth holding it all together.

LIVING IN THE SPACE OF LIGHT

The lines, which comprise this grid, in theory or in fact, are often referred to as "Ley Lines." When we study them closely, we see that humans throughout recorded history appear to have been well aware of their existence, thanks to the many ancient sites found along them. The term "Ley" itself comes from the Anglo-Saxon, meaning, "cleared strips of ground" or "meadows." But these lines we are referring to are primarily energetic, and exist whether the land is stripped of its ground cover or not.

All Ley Lines meet at intersecting points, forming a matrix or grid across the body of the planet. These grid points, according to proponents, are the strongest "power spots" on Earth. Apparently many of our ancestors thought so too, since sacred sites such as henges, mounds, megaliths, pyramids, famous energy vortexes, and even cathedrals are frequently located directly atop these cross-hair power spots.

Mapping the grid shows us that many of the world's most renowned sites sit atop Ley Line meeting points. Machu Picchu, the Pyramids of Giza, Easter Island, Puma Punku, Lhasa Tibet, the ancient ruins of Mohenjo Daro, Findhorn in Scotland, the Bermuda Triangle, the Arizona vortices, Angkor Wat, the Nazca Lines, numerous obelisks, and sacred domed structures around the globe all attest to the very real possibility that something beyond the visible world is involved here.

A grid network is reflected as a deep organizing principle throughout the universe—from the way that galaxies cluster together, to the way that our DNA spirals in its perfected form. A crystalline matrix of light is restructuring our auric fields to take on the form of an octahedral diamond—two pyramids joined base to base. Our personal energy fields require alignment to this form through the architecture of the diamond.

The same strength that the diamond shaped energy grid brings to your energy fields, enabling you to hold and utilize far higher quantities of supercharged, high frequency energy, also strengthens your emotional, mental and physical bodies providing you with the means at all levels to expand and evolve to the mineral aspects of hardness, brightness and translucence that make the diamond a symbol of perfection, while holding your personal space with a greater degree of balance and authentic power.

The diamond grid is the vehicle for recalibrating you to your highest expression and the energy of your soul. It is your conduit to Source and an embodiment of the heart of all that is. You are a part of this ever-strengthening grid of light weaving its form across the planet. Take up your place, and tap in to this original diamond blueprint to co-create a more harmonious world.

I have been living on top of a hill in the south of Johannesburg for a very long time. The view from there is almost 360 degrees. The little bit that is not visible from my home can be seen from going around the block or when I drive down the hill to the shops. I have built a huge column of light for the city of Johannesburg from that hill. It started with my childlike practice of sending light to my area and the people who need light to a conscious intention to establish a light grid that will enable Johannesburg to become a city of light. It has been my silent purpose for over thirty years.

Over the years many things started changing in South Africa and the world over. By that time the diamond form of the grid must have been well established, but I got a sense that the grid needed to be stabilised. I prayed for guidance, and as it has always been in my life, God showed me how to ground my light into the earth and to align it with the heavens and stars. I had to build a column of light that went deep into the earth and high into the sky, almost like a lighthouse that could send signals out, visible from very far.

Typical with my nature, I loved to play around with the idea and made such a huge column of light that I was sure NASA became aware of it. I knew there must have been others like me, placed strategically over the world to light up the grid. It gave me intense pleasure to think how these pillars of light must have puzzled NASA and to imagine they knew about me!

The practice of sending light became more structured as my consciousness grew. I was introduced to the power of pyramids after I travelled to Egypt. The power of two pyramids placed base to base, or the octahedron, became the tool I used to grid energy. My columns of light became octahedrons of light, and I could feel that the energy was more balanced and much more powerful.

Julie Umpleby, a friend of mine, then came up with channelled information about a diamond light grid and diamond codes. I loved her work because my octahedrons of light made more sense then, and by doing her workshops I was empowered with tools to strengthen my own grid by using the shape of a diamond.

I was still silently doing my light work. I played around with what she taught me in my healing practice and was stunned by the results! The positive feedback from my patients was inspiring. I started using it on my dogs, and they rewarded me with curious looks, better behaviour, and better health. I started drawing diamonds around things I felt needed more balance. Sometimes I could see immediate results, and other times I could see nothing. I kept on practicing and had loads of fun with it. My intention was always for the good of all of God's creation. It became standard practice in times of crisis or chaos.

One year, while on vacation in Mozambique, there was a fire in the resort where we stayed. The fire spread to a bungalow of friends, and suddenly the whole resort was under threat of burning down to the ground. A strong wind came up, and the fire spread to another bungalow. Everyone was frantic, and I watched my family taking control of the group, creating a strategy to deal with the crisis.

I watched my children fighting the fire, putting their own lives at risk. I stood quietly in the middle of it all, praying God would protect them and stop the fire. It became instinctive behaviour to draw diamonds around every person and every bungalow, a diamond around the resort, a diamond around every structure that was on fire. The wind was howling, and I saw the grass roof of another bungalow catching fire. It was quickly put out by my sons, who were already on the roof, throwing buckets of water on the thatch to protect it from catching fire.

I realised the wind created a huge threat to the destruction of the entire resort. I had never before used the diamond grid on the elements but had a sense it was needed. I put my hand up and started drawing a huge diamond with my index finger around the wind in the sky. It was the first time ever that I used my hand in a visible way. With a hushed voice, I talked to the wind and asked it to please be calm, to hush, hush, hush.

Within a few minutes, the wind calmed down completely to a very gentle breeze. I scanned the area around me, and through the smoke I saw a young friend of my children who had been running around frantically, carrying possessions out of burning buildings, come to a standstill with his hand up in the air, like mine, urging the wind to be calm. His actions were unconscious, I saw as I looked into his wild, uncomprehending eyes.

With the wind calm and all the people working together as a team, it was easy to put the fire out and save the resort. Afterwards we all sat together quietly and in gratitude that no lives were lost and that the holiday would carry on for most of us as if nothing had ever happened. The only reminder was four black ruins in the far corner of the resort.

What a powerful experience to teach me that even the elements can and will obey! I was reminded of the parable of Jesus in the stormy sea and how he asked the sea to calm down and it did. Jesus said over and over again that we have the same power as he did and more. I take those words with trust and faith, and I use my diamond grid on anyone or anything that needs balance in this world. I also pray that my action will not interfere with the path of the other; the only purpose is to create a state of balance.

The fire in Mozambique gave me faith and courage to work with nature. In Johannesburg we have fierce thunderstorms and lightning. We often have flash floods that can create havoc on the roads in our city and can leave many living in informal settlements homeless. I draw my diamonds with love and gratitude to balance the energies of the elements and to protect fellow citizens of our country. Practise makes perfect, and the more I practise the quicker the balancing takes place. Prevention is better than cure, and often the balancing is started as soon as the sky becomes heavy and dangerous looking. It doesn't stop the rain, but it calms the elemental energies so they do not become a combined force that destroys everything that gets in its way.

This exercise has also taught me that everything in our Universe reacts to geometry, even our bodies. It makes me calm a takes the fear out of me. It enables me to take control and to view every situation in love and gratitude. The atoms recognise and respond to the geometry and the perfection in which it was created.

I believe every person who crosses my path each day is there for a reason, and I take full responsibility for that. I also know this works both ways. We

LIVING IN THE SPACE OF LIGHT

are equally important in each other's lives. I choose to make it a memorable occasion for both of us. When we brush shoulders, we mix our energies. It is almost like baking a cake: get the right ingredients together—you and me in this moment—and mix the ingredients in a suitable way, as the recipe requires, ensuring the perfect outcome for this moment.

Some of us just pass briefly There is no time to do icing and put the cherry on top, but we still have the opportunity to bake a perfect cake together. Give light, and give love in the moment to raise your own vibration by opening your heart. Shower others with light and love by opening your heart to them. Often the others will feel something happening in their bodies and will raise their eyes to make contact with you. That moment when the eyes meet and are locked in silence is a joyful moment in the Universe. The angels sing and play their harps to celebrate the joining of two souls in a moment of oneness.

Practise this when you walk in the streets or when you drive past pedestrians on your way to work. Let your intention always be to cause no harm, to treat self and others with loving-kindness and compassion while seeking true happiness. It is a good exercise to control impatience when you stand in a queue or in a boardroom where the energies are not flowing well.

It is important to centre and ground yourself before you do this. Feet planted firmly on the ground, feel the energy of the earth moving up through your legs, and feel energy from your body going into the earth. Lengthen your spine by pulling your neck long, like a puppet on a string. Tuck the chin in slightly. Gather yourself towards your centre of gravity, two fingers below your belly button.

Visualise the geometric shape of the octahedron around you. The shape of a diamond with four equal sides or two pyramids base to base. Visualise how you place yourself inside your diamond. Check that you fit in properly, no limbs hanging out anywhere, and see that you are able to move about comfortably in your diamond. If you keep on getting a visual image of you standing on your head or bunched up in one corner, it tells you more about your alignment and the restrictions it causes in your life.

Take time to practise how to fit into your diamond perfectly and to move inside it comfortably. You are going to use this exercise on others as well,

— 53 —

and if you cannot align yourself it will be impossible to align others in their diamonds.

This exercise can be used to handle conflict or to improve relationships. It offers a way to centre, ground, and balance yourself and others. If we interact from a place of balance and from a point of central reference for everyone involved, emotions will be more controlled, communication will be clearer, and the need to defend or lash out will be less—in general the situation can unfold in a space of balance and harmony.

You choose if you want to be aligned in your own diamond, or do you feel like inviting the other person into your diamond? There will be times where it will be difficult to get two people aligned in one diamond. Make sure the intention of creating balance through love and gratitude is clear at all times. Sometimes you will not get two people in one diamond because the other person is not ready to share that space with anyone. Honour the free will of the person—you cannot force your intention on anyone. Rather, assist him or her to find balance within his or her own sacred space of the diamond.

Remember all this work is done in your thoughts, with your mind's eye, and all communication is done through the spirit. The other person is not consciously aware of what you are doing, although we are all connected on a spiritual level. You may just find a more relaxed demeanour or calmness entering the situation. When you do this, your intention not to manipulate or to meddle in someone else's affairs must be clear. You must believe in what you are doing, and you must trust that the outcome will be in the best interest of all involved.

I use a diamond to grid my challenges, problems, and projects, and I fill the diamond with gratitude. I bless our food this way, protect our property and possessions, and protect our pets and wild animals. I use the diamond shape to heal my own body. I use a diamond to heal patients, plants, and animals.

Our family breed wild buck species on a farm about 250 kilometres from Johannesburg. We spend most of our weekends there to care for the animals and to connect with nature. We love the animals and have close connections with a few specific ones. The giraffes are my special animals and it is my dream to start a giraffe sanctuary there.

I have a baby giraffe called Laa La who lost her mother at the tender age of five months. The loss of her mother, Chi Chi, left a huge imprint of trauma on my life, and to this day I find it difficult to know she is no longer around. After Chi Chi's death, we were not sure Laa La would survive, as giraffes nurse from their mothers for a year. Jo Jo, her father, kept a close eye on her but could do nothing to save her. She had to eat on her own.

Bittersweet emotions rushed through me when we watched her eating the new tender, green leaves from the acacia trees. She was going to be all right! Jo Jo stayed around to keep Laa La company for about a year before he jumped the fence to the neighbouring farm to find new company. My heart was broken all over again, but I knew it was what he wanted and what was best for him. In my mind I drew a diamond around him to protect him and sent him off in love.

Laa La then started walking with the wildebeests to keep her company, and she even picked up jumping and charging from them. They allowed her into their group, but nature still followed its own way, and one day we noticed a very long and deep gash in her upper thigh, just below the buttock, where a wildebeest had gaffed her. She clearly needed to be checked out by a vet. The vet told us it is very dangerous to dart giraffes, and she had a 50 percent chance to survive. Heartbreak all over again! I did not want to take that chance.

I took charge of the situation. My husband and I followed Laa La in the Land Rover, and I drew diamonds around her and around her wound while I prayed for healing. I lay in my bed at night, two hundred kilometres away from the farm, and did distant healing, in the same way as on the farm but in my mind.

The following weekend on the farm, Laa La showed no signs of discomfort. She walked without a limp, and the wound looked considerably smaller. I did diamond healing for two weeks, and when we saw her again the wound was closed, and she looked healthy as could be!

When I use the shape of the diamond, my intention is to bring balance and harmony through love and gratitude. I think of it as bringing my prayer, held within the diamond, to God. I then leave it in God's hands, entrusting it totally to Him. With faith I know that God knows best, and I step away without expectations of what the outcome must be.

8

DIAMONDS ARE FOREVER

OUR JOURNEY HERE on earth has its own cause. We have free will to choose how we want to live here; we have the ability to change our state constantly. It can be compared to the difference of state between graphite and a diamond. Carbon is the main element in organic matter. Carbon atoms are the only element in both graphite and diamond. The element carbon is not found in a pure form in the human body but rather in compounds within the body. Carbon constitutes roughly 18 percent of body mass, and millions of carbon atoms form the thousands of molecules in virtually every cell. Carbon is the basic building block required to form proteins, carbohydrates, and fats, and it plays a crucial role in regulating the physiology of the body. Every living organism contains carbon in some way or another.

The word *diamond* comes from the Greek word *adamas*, meaning "indestructible." The strongest material known to man, a diamond, consists purely of carbon, making it the only gem comprised of a single element (it consists of 99.95 percent carbon). Found in abundance, carbon takes on many forms: the difference between a diamond and a lump of coal is essentially their molecular structures.

Diamonds are considered the world's oldest treasure, having formed over 3.3 billion years ago, two hundred kilometres below the earth's surface. Under conditions of intense heat (nine hundred to thirteen hundred degrees Celsius) and pressure (between forty-five and sixty kilo bars), carbon atoms crystallise, forming diamonds. It takes millions of years for a diamond to form, and geologists believe the most recently formed diamonds may be up to 45 million years old. Variations of temperature and pressure can significantly impact the formation of diamonds, and if the conditions are not ideal, it could result in the dissolution of the diamonds.

Diamonds, being perfect forms of carbon, are the purest expression of earth's energy. Diamonds are also connected with the nonphysical planes, as evidenced by their unparalleled ability to refract light of all colours. Thus the diamond is a bridge or link between the physical and spiritual realms. Diamonds are great conductors of energy, both physically and spiritually. Diamonds symbolise truth.

Coal or charcoal has an amorphous structure. All the carbon atoms have strong chemical bonds to three other carbon atoms, making sheets that look like chicken wire; weak forces hold the sheets together in stacks that can slide past each other easily. When you're writing with a pencil on paper, these sheets are sliding apart to leave the graphite chunks behind as marks on the paper. Like diamonds, coal is also formed deep within the earth's crust.

Diamonds have a crystalline structure, which resembles the shape of two pyramids joined at the base. When a diamond is formed, each of its carbon atoms bonds with another four carbon atoms, making perfect tetrahedra on and on throughout the crystal. This means each atom is essentially participating in four extremely strong covalent bonds. As a result of these bonds, diamonds are fifty-eight times harder than any other matter found in nature.

A diamond in its rough form has potential, its size simply a promise of what it might be. Only in the hands of master craftsmen does a diamond reach its true potential. By using the analogy of a diamond to describe the value of each man, woman, and child, regardless of externals, every person is a true diamond, the toughest substance in existence. Everyone has a pure soul, and regardless of behaviour and outward appearance, every soul remains intact. Unconquerable.

The pure soul descended into a material world to demonstrate its power and glory to illuminate the universe. The soul was uprooted from its natural

LIVING IN THE SPACE OF LIGHT

spiritual habitat and embedded the diamond-soul in the hard rock of harsh materialism, under layers upon layers that initially shroud and obscure the fire and brilliance, and even the very existence of the soul.

Our immersion in material survival makes it difficult for us to recognise our inherent spirituality. The majority of our time—more than twenty tons of rock compared to one diamond—is preoccupied with work, eating, sleeping, paying our bills, and entertaining us. No wonder our inexperienced eyes don't see diamonds.

The trained eye sees the diamonds in others. To fulfil its purpose, a diamond needs to be excavated, cut, and polished. This is the mission with which every one of us has been charged.

The first step is gaining the awareness that in the hard rock is hidden a precious diamond. We must identify the diamond quality and reach for it with unconditional love. The second step is excavation and cutting: clearing away the externals and allowing the diamond to emerge. To reveal the diamond in a raw world of rock requires peeling away the outer layers, shedding unrefined habits, eliminating the inappropriate—allowing for the diamond to surface. Some stones need to be sawed, others cleaved. They then need to be rounded out and polished, and finally this process yields the completed diamond that radiates and beautifies this world.

Every diamond-soul has its own unique personality, its strengths (carats), clarity, colour, and cut—and it must be treated in kind, befitting its personal individuality. Each stone needs to be cut precisely, with the greatest sensitivity, a most beautiful cut uniquely appropriate for this particular stone. Everyone is a diamond; we must wait patiently, untiringly, because this tenacious attitude will bring the diamond to the surface. We must recognise that all people are diamonds and help actualise every individual's precious potential by excavating, cutting, and polishing and revealing the brilliance within, allowing every man, woman, and child's inner personality to emerge and illuminate the world in which we live.

Mineral aspects of hardness, brightness, and translucence make the diamond a symbol of perfection. In Western tradition the diamond is the symbol of universal sovereignty, of incorruptibility and absolute truth. In

— 59 —

Renaissance art the diamond symbolises equanimity, courage in the face of adversity, the power to free the spirit from every fear, integrity of character, and good faith.

A diamond contains innocence, wisdom, and faithfulness. In the language of iconography, the diamond is the symbol of constancy, strength, and other heroic virtues, radiating the divine. The diamond symbolises perfection in its solidity and near indestructibility. From this the diamond becomes a symbol of strength in a physical sense and righteousness in a spiritual sense. It equally represents truth and strength. The two are considered cognates since the truth means nothing without the strength to fight for it.

The geometry of a diamond is an octahedron, a three-dimensional object composed of one- and two-dimensional parts. These parts have special names. The base of an octahedron is a square. If you picture an octahedron as two congruent square pyramids that have their bottoms touching, then the base of the octahedron is the square between the two pyramids. An octahedron has eight faces, which are all in the shape of equilateral triangles. These eight faces are where the solid gets its name—*octa* means eight. These faces form the surface area of the octahedron. The square that is the base of the octahedron is not part of the surface area; therefore, the base is not also a face.

When two faces touch, the line segment that is formed is called an edge. An octahedron has twelve edges. When two edges intersect, they form a vertex (plural being *vertices*). The octahedron has six vertices. Each vertex is formed when four edges intersect. The octahedron form represents the merging of the physical, mental, and spiritual planes, thus symbolising a state of completion. The octahedron, or double pyramid, was a key factor in reaching oneness or enlightenment. The octahedron is the "golden key" to uniting all parts of the time continuum existing within the cosmic/human heart.

Octahedron consciousness was predominant upon earth during some very ancient and enlightened civilisations. But in our past, as our planet more fully explored the experience of polarity, the octahedron teachings were known by only few, if at all. Now that a planetary change in consciousness is occurring, we can use the tools known deep inside of us and by the ancients to uplift our energies and continue the process of spiritual integration.

LIVING IN THE SPACE OF LIGHT

We use the four sides of the diamond of our being to learn more about ourselves, to learn about other beings, and to express ourselves creatively in the world. The design of a diamond or of any gemstone must be symmetrical about an axis, for symmetry and regularity in the disposition of the facets are essential for a pleasing result. It works the same way with us, and life is a constant search to find equilibrium, always seeking alignment and balance in situations that challenge us.

We align vertically anchored between God and earth—"as above, so below." In this state we are more relaxed, receptive, and able to hear our souls' guidance. We remember we are larger than any circumstances around us. We are able to stay balanced and resourceful. We can take inspired action no matter what challenges life brings us. We feel calm, safe, and held, unaffected by the chaos of the external world. We remember we are not alone. We are able to deal with whatever comes our way and handle our life responsibilities with greater grace and ease. We move from just surviving to thriving and feel more fulfilled from the inside out. It shifts us out of the confusion and overwhelm of our external world into the clarity and equanimity of our true diamond self within. It makes us feel more alive and more passionate.

We align horizontally to explore self and what keeps us happy and safe, expanding in the horizontal direction in material possessions or pleasures and what effects they have on us. That point of individual identity in us called the self has direct access and simultaneous communication with each of the four sides of our human nature—physical, emotional, mental, and spiritual. We have the power to integrate the four sides of our being into a harmonious, functioning whole as well as the power to use our creativity for the progress of the community in which we live.

We align spatially to be in touch with our own divinity. We possess divine individuality, which recognises its oneness with the creator and with all life. We all sprang from the same source. But each of us is unique, different, and has a unique gift to give to humanity.

Each of us is like a facet of the diamond mind of God, a hue of God's light, and a note in the symphony called life. We are all one, but we are not the same. Embracing our divinity means embracing our divine individuality and living it—being it here on earth. The human being is a symbol, a mirror, and an expression of the perfection of divinity. Every aspect in our being, call it psychological or substantial, reveals a facet of the divine whole. It is our free will to decide how much of our divine perfection we want to reveal to the world.

The law of rebound concerns the right of one to come out of a negative situation stronger and bolder and with more soul growth than previously experienced. This has been used as an example in stories since the beginning of mankind. Traumatic situations create the need for rebound, and the soul often seeks these negative occurrences to give self and observers a leap in faith.

Diamond cutting and polishing is the process of transforming a rough diamond into a brilliant, faceted display of light. It is an art and an exact science that requires intense precision, attention to detail and state-of-the-art technology. It takes years of experience and training to acquire the skills needed for this process, as every facet must be perfectly aligned in order to ensure the mesmerizing brilliance and sparkle you see in diamonds. Even the smallest of mistakes can have a major impact on the quality of the cut of the final gem.

We are all diamond cutters. How appropriate that only a diamond can cut a diamond. Only one soul can reach another. No machines, no other powerful forces can do the job. Take the strongest body, the strongest material force, and you can cut and shape any other piece of matter. But not a diamond. The physical body cannot touch the ethereal spirit. A soul, on the other hand, even if it is only soul dust, can reach and touch another soul with love.

In a diamond the amount of light reflected from the surface is much smaller than that penetrating into the stone. A diamond is practically perfectly transparent, so all the light that passes into the stone has to pass out again. This is why lustre may be ignored in the working out of the correct shape for a diamond and why any variation in the amount of light reflected from the exposed surface due to a change in that surface may be considered negligible in the calculations.

The brilliancy, or, as it is sometimes termed, the fire or the life of a gem thus depends entirely upon the play of light in the gem, upon the path of rays of light in the gem. If a gem is so cut or designed that every ray of light passing into it follows the best path possible for producing pleasing effects upon the eye, then the gem is perfectly cut. The whole art of the lapidary consists in proportioning his stone and disposing his facets so as to ensure this result.

A gem, not being in itself a source of light, cannot shine with other than reflected light. The maximum amount of light will be given off by the gem if the whole of the light that strikes it is reflected by the back of the gem—by that part hidden by the setting—and sent out into the air by its front part. The facets of the stone must therefore be so disposed that no light that enters it is let out through its back but that it is wholly reflected. This result is obtained by having the facets inclined in such a way that all the light that strikes them does so at an angle of incidence greater than the critical angle.

When the soul becomes divine it becomes a diamond, reflecting the divine light and forming an aura of delicate tints around itself. Such is the perfect Human Soul the human soul aspires towards perfection.

—PETER DEUNOV

The cut of a diamond refers not to its shape, but to the balance of proportion, symmetry and polish achieved by the diamond cutter. The extent of how well the diamond is cut is directly related to the diamond's overall beauty. When a diamond has been correctly cut, the diamond's ability to reflect and refract light is greatly enhanced. By understanding the way that light moves through diamond crystals, modern diamond cutters have established a specific set of proportions and angles that are known to harness the diamond's internal brilliance and to show it in its best light.

Cut is considered to be the most important of all of the diamond characteristics, as a well-cut diamond will often appear larger than a poorly cut diamond of the same carat weight, and have the appearance of enhanced colour and clarity. The quality of cut is determined by how well the symmetry, polish and proportions of the diamond produce the most attractive balance of the three different types of reflection. Several proportion factors have the most immediate impact on a diamond's ability to reflect light correctly. The table size and depth of a diamond relative to the diameter greatly impacts the light return from a diamond. A well-cut diamond is proportioned so that most of the light entering the gem exits backs through the top of the stone, perfectly balancing the white light (brilliance) with intense flashes of fire (dispersion). A poorly cut diamond, with facets cut only a few degrees out of alignment, can result in light exiting through the bottom of the diamond, known as light leakage, instead of from the top where it is visible. This creates a diamond with dulled brilliance from poor light performance within the gem, making the centre of the gem look dark.

It is to light, the play of light, its reflection, and its refraction that a gem owes its brilliancy, its fire, and its colour, and so do we.

9

THE ALCHEMIST

The Law of Healing concerns the ability of one to channel energy (prana—chi—holy spirit) that radiates from the Source we call God. The purpose of this channelled energy is to either improve self or another by removing blockages or instilling the sacred energy, which pulsates from the Source of God. With intent or technique we may send this energy to the past, present, or future. Hands-on healers who are effective in healing have brain waves at 7.8 Hz—the same as the earth's pulse beat. Their brain waves are in sync with the earths at the time the healing is performed. Another aspect of this law is the ability of one in third dimension to heal self by that, which triggers a leap in faith.

The Law of Higher Will. From the viewpoint of our separate self and smaller will, it's normal to act on the basis of our own desires and preferences. When we surrender our smaller self and will to the guidance of a higher will and dedicate our actions for the highest good of ALL concerned, we feel an inspired glow at the centre of our life.

For CENTURIES, ALCHEMISTS have sought to change base metals into gold. But the transmutation of metals like lead into gold is actually symbolic of a higher and nobler alchemy—the alchemy of self-transformation. SELF-TRANSFORMATION was the goal of the most spiritual of alchemists. They sought a way to change the lead of negative human energy into the gold of divine energy, and some of them achieved this by using the violet flame. The violet flame (also called the violet fire) is a unique spiritual energy that can help you in all areas of your life. It can heal emotional and physical problems, improve your relationships, and help you to grow spiritually, or just make life easier.

The flame is the essence of a unique spiritual light. Mystics of all ages have glimpsed a spiritual spectrum behind the physical spectrum. Radiant colours, more pure and rare than those found on earth, emanate from a brilliant, inner divine light. Just as a ray of sunlight passing through a prism refracts into seven colours, spiritual light splits into seven colours, or rays—each of which has specific divine qualities. The violet flame comes forth from the violet ray, which has the qualities of mercy, forgiveness, freedom and transmutation. The colour violet has long been associated with spirituality. Having the highest frequency in the visible spectrum, violet is at the point of transition to the next octave of light.

To the ancients, this transcendental colour was a spiritual rather than a physical phenomenon. Saints and adepts throughout the ages have known how to use the violet flame. The violet flame has the power to erase, or transmute the cause, the effect, and even the memory of our past mistakes. Transmutation means to change—to alter in form, appearance or nature. The violet flame changes negative energy into positive energy, darkness into light, and "fate" into opportunity.

Our past actions—both good and bad come back to us. This impersonal cosmic law decrees that whatever we do comes full circle to our doorstep for resolution; simply, what goes around comes around. The violet flame is able to transmute or mitigate our negative karma before it comes back to us.

On the physical level, the violet flame can help our bodies to heal by removing what makes us vulnerable to illness and disease. The real cause of disease is often rooted in our mental, emotional and spiritual states.

Today, we are discovering more and more about how our thoughts and emotions can affect our health. Research has shown that hatred and other

LIVING IN THE SPACE OF LIGHT

negative thoughts and feelings actually create excess amounts of acid that the body cannot assimilate. These negative thoughts and feelings often originate in emotional and psychological problems, which the violet flame can help to resolve.

The scars of old hurts and painful memories may be healed and dissolved when the healing balm of the violet flame is applied. The violet flame works by changing "vibrations." In physics, vibration is the speed of oscillation—the speed at which something moves back and forth. On the atomic level, vibration can be understood to be the speed at which electrons orbit around the nucleus of the atom. The violet flame works by changing vibrations on this level.

Atoms are mostly empty space. The empty space between the nucleus and the electrons is where negative energy can become stuck. When the atoms in our bodies and auras become clogged with this negativity, the electrons whirl slower and slower, and we begin to resonate more with negativity and less with light. It lowers vibration. The violet flame transmutes this negative energy. Because there is less density within the atom, the electrons whirl faster and faster, thereby raising the vibration. When you have a higher vibration, there is more spiritual energy in your body. Acupuncturists and energetic healers know that optimum health comes when this spiritual energy flows freely throughout the body. The violet flame frees up this energy and re-establishes harmony and equilibrium, propelling you into a more spiritual state of being.

The violet flame is a tool of self-transformation. Physical experiments in alchemy whereby base metals are transformed into gold are symbolic of what the violet flame does. In medieval times, alchemists attempted to transmute base metals into gold, using heat to separate the "subtle" from the "gross." While there have always been alchemists who sought to create wealth by transmuting base metals, this process of transmutation is symbolic of a higher and more noble alchemy—the alchemy of self-transformation.

Alchemists of the Spirit did not seek physical wealth, but spiritual wealth. They sought to transform themselves into more spiritual beings, by becoming more loving, wise and compassionate. The violet flame has the capacity to bring about this transformation by transmuting negative elements within us. It has the unique ability to transform fear into courage, anxiety into peace and hatred into love.

Alchemists of all ages have sought the mystical philosophers' stone. Early alchemists pored over minutely ciphered texts in search of this stone. For them, it was worth a lifetime to decode the mystery of this "stone" which symbolized the transmutation of the lower animal nature into the highest and divine. The coveted philosophers' stone—"the stone which is no stone"—was not physical, but spiritual, and created out of fire.]

Some alchemists did discover the secret of the violet flame. According to Neo-Platonist alchemists, the philosophers' stone was a self-transforming fire that would lead their souls upward, by drawing up to the Spirit all qualities which dragged downward and opposed the spiritual essences. In the process, the "hard and refractory materials" in their bodies would be transmuted into a rare and more luminous material. In this sacred experiment, they said the alchemist would pursue "the gold of the wise and not the vulgar metal." Transmutation, then, was not just a process that turned base metals into gold, but also a spiritual process that raised the soul into a state of unity.

Its action is to transmute denser feelings, actions, deeds, karma, and so on into a higher vibrational frequency. You may use the Violet Flame in perfect harmony with any belief system, religion or practice. It is a neutral tool with absolutely no conditions attached to it.

Find a place where you won't be disturbed, and sit comfortably in a straight chair with your spine and head erect, legs and arms uncrossed and feet flat on the floor. Rest your hands on your upper legs, with palms facing upwards. The violet flame is invoked through "decreeing"—a unique form of spoken prayer utilizing visualization and meditation.

One of the simplest decrees to the violet flame is: "I AM a being of violet fire! I AM the purity God desires!" Take a few, slow deep breathes and centre in your heart. Start out slowly, giving the decree with love, devotion and feeling. Repeating the decree strengthens its power and draws down more light.

Once you are familiar with the decree, you can close your eyes while giving it and concentrate on visualizing the violet flame. See yourself before a

LIVING IN THE SPACE OF LIGHT

large bonfire, about nine feet high and six feet wide. Colour it violet in your imagination, and see the flames pulsating and undulating in endless shades of violet with gradations of purple and pink. Then see yourself stepping into the flame, so the violet flame is where you physically are. See your body as transparent, with the flames curling up from beneath your feet, passing through and around your body, clear up over your head. Often the words of a violet flame decree invoke ideas for other violet flame visualizations—decreeing is meant to be fun so be creative and use your imagination!

You can use the violet flame to help family and friends. Just visualize the violet flame around them while you give the decree, and add a prayer before you start. The violet flame can help others that you might not be aware of. After you have finished decreeing, you can ask: "In the name of the Christ within me, I ask that this violet flame be multiplied and used to assist all souls on this planet who are in need. I thank you and accept it done according to the will of God."

Even a few minutes of violet flame will produce results, but persistence is needed to penetrate age-old habits you would like to change. You can start out with just a few minutes of violet flame in the morning to help you through the day, and you can add the violet flame to whatever prayers or meditations you currently practice.

You can use the violet flame and experience the healing, transformation and spiritual upliftment. The Violet Flame is a Divine gift and tool for everyone. People with the gift of interdimensional sight have seen it. Cameras have captured it when it was not visible to the person taking the photo. The Violet Flame is REAL. There are unlimited ways to use the Violet Flame.

Step 1. Bring the Violet Flame into your body. It is helpful to visualize (doesn't matter if you can or cannot actually see it) or pretend that there is a ball of violet fire above your head. Then ask that ball of fire to come into your body and fill every speck of your entire body.

Step 2. Spin the flame in and around your body. Keep the Flame inside your body while asking it to also come out through your heart chakra and spin around or encircle the outside of your body so that it's encompassing your emotional, mental and spiritual bodies.

Step 3. The intention is to transmute everything you wish to be changed or eliminated from your life. Some people like to mention everything like a shopping list—all karma, negative feelings such as anger, poverty, frustration, sadness, physical illnesses, and so on, which is fine. But you can also do a catchall phrase, such as "transmute anything and everything standing in the way of my becoming a Christed Being."

Again, it's the intent and the feeling behind it. Add the phrase "on all dimensions, on all levels, through all time and space, past, present and future" to your request.

Step 4. Change negativity into Divine Light and fill your body. Energy is never lost nor can it be "deleted," however, it can be CHANGED into a higher frequency. That is why it is important to ask the Violet Flame to do so. You can specify what the energy is to become. Then call that new energy into your body and aura. Some people like to do the list again. "Please transmute everything into love, prosperity, abundance, peace and happiness."

You can ask for specific colour rays, which are pure energy. Pink is unconditional love. Blue is peace and tranquillity. Green is health and abundance. Deep dark blue is spiritual knowledge and intuition. Violet is spiritual advancement and knowledge. The Violet Flame Invocation below turns everything into the Golden Platinum light of the Christ Consciousness, which encompasses all the qualities of the other colours.

Once you understand the process, please individualise the Invocation using words from your heart and say them with great feeling and intention. Saying the words out loud is best because the power and vibration of the spoken word has energy, which helps create the maximum results of the Violet Flame. If you are among people that would not understand your words, you can say it quietly in your mind.

Centre yourself. Take a few deep breaths to prepare, and then say:

Mighty I AM Presence, Beloved God, My Heavenly Source, Please make manifest in me now the Sacred Violet Flame of Transmutation. Bring the Violet Flame into every cell, molecule and atom of my body filling me totally and completely.

Blessed Violet Flame blaze into my Heart and expand out and around all of my bodies, physical, emotional, mental and spiritual, surrounding my entire Being with your Divine Grace, Love, Mercy and Forgiveness.

Transmute all karma, negative thoughts, actions, deeds and energy that I have ever created at any time, in all dimensions, on all levels, in all bodies, through all time and space, past, present and future, for all Eternity. Transmute anything and everything that stands in my way of embodying the Ascended Christ Being That I AM.

Beloved Violet Flame turn all that has been transmuted Into the Golden Platinum Light of God, the Christ Consciousness, The Light of God that never fails.

Send this Golden Platinum Light to me now, filling and surrounding my entire body with its Divine Radiance. Raise my vibration and frequency to the highest level possible for me at this time.

So Be It and So It Is. Thank You God. Amen.

It is suggested that you do this first thing in the morning and last thing at night, or anytime you feel a little overwhelmed or upset. Just Violet Flame what is going on, right then and there.

A few years ago I got an e-mail from a questionable source to inform me that the government was planning to enforce a toll system on existing roads in Gauteng. I felt rebellious about the idea because the taxpayers already paid for the roads. The whole scheme lacked integrity, and I refused to support it at all. It was kept from the public, and the fact that I received the e-mail was no coincidence. I searched for my truth about the project and found myself getting more rebellious about it. I started discussing it with friends and like-minded people and found we shared the same views.

I meditated and prayed about it and was shown to treat the problem with integrity—thus love and gratitude. I put the scheme and all involved with it in a diamond to bring balance to it. A small group of friends and I blazed the violet flame to clear out negativity that was attached to the project. We joined forces by sending light, love, and gratitude to the project.

Despite the work we did to stop the project for two years before the public got notified, the project went ahead. The public also reacted rebelliously.

Obviously a bigger picture needed to be played out. We watched calmly as tollgates and toll stations were erected on the highways of Gauteng.

It was extremely interesting to see that the buildings had windows in the shape of diamonds and the tollgates were zigzag rows, which gave the appearance of diamonds as you approached. I would love to think the diamond grid exercise inspired the designing engineers! It was really funny when the project was finished and the lights at the tollgates were switched on, and they were violet! They created cleansing stations for the people of Gauteng.

I called the group to gather again so I could share the good news. We sat together and said prayers of gratitude. With the intention of love and gratitude, we initiated the tollgates as our very special cleansing stations. Every person who drives through a tollgate is balanced by the diamond grid and cleansed by the violet flame. How more blessed can we be? I am not sure if there are any other cities in the world that bless their citizens with diamond grids and violet flames.

To date the tollgate project has not been able to generate the income the government wished for because most citizens are refusing to pay the toll fees. Unknowingly, citizens receive two powerful blessings every time they cross a tollgate.

The goal of our work was to stop the toll road project for lack of integrity; our intention was to bring balance, love, and gratitude to it. God transformed it into something beyond our expectation, which shows the utmost integrity for the good of all.

When a person's intention is held in the mind and the action of the physical effort does not follow, a false impression of self is created. Energy must follow intention for good to happen. When an act of kindness is performed and the intention is to be recognised for goodness, or if there is an underlying motivation that is not of the higher order, integrity is at stake. Intention and effort must be of a higher vibration to gain or create spiritual accomplishment and reward. If a person gives a promise to another to do something, and has an intention to do so, but does no action to fulfil the promise, it becomes a lie, a breaking of one's word, and creates karma.

LIVING IN THE SPACE OF LIGHT

An intention is a clear and positive statement of an outcome you want to experience. Your intentions influence your actual experiences. An intention is not oriented toward a future outcome. It is a path or practice that is focused on how you are being in the present moment. Your attention is on the ever-present now in the constantly changing flow of life. You set your intentions based on understanding what matters most to you and make a commitment to align your worldly actions with your inner values.

When you gain insight through meditation, wise reflection, and moral living, your ability to act from your intentions blossoms. It is called a practice because it is an ever-renewing process. You don't just set your intentions and then forget about them; you live them every day.

My basic intention is to cause no harm and to treat others and myself with loving-kindness and compassion while seeking true happiness. I am committing to living each moment with the intention of not causing harm with my actions and words and not violating others through my livelihood or sexuality. I am connecting to my own sense of kindness and innate dignity. On this ground of intention, I am then able to participate as I choose in life's contests, until I outgrow them.

Goals help you make your place in the world and be an effective person. But intention is what provides integrity and unity in your life. Intention is what provides you with self-respect and peace of mind. Through the skilful cultivation of intention, you learn to make wise goals and then to work hard toward achieving them without getting caught in attachment to outcome.

Right intention is like a muscle—you develop it over time by exercising it. When you lose it, you just start over again. There's no need to judge yourself or quit when you fail to live by your intentions. You are developing the habit of right intention so it becomes an unconscious way of living—an automatic response to all situations. Right intention is organic; it thrives when cultivated and wilts when neglected.

— 73 —

10

A CHRISTED BEING

WE ALL COME to earth with powerful gifts to offer. These gifts will help us to unlock the divine in us or to become Christ like. We choose if we want to make use of these gifts because God gave us free will to create our own lives on our earthly journey. If we do not search for excellence within, we refuse the unrecognised or unrealised gifts within.

We can get in touch with our own source of intuition and wisdom only when we no longer depend on others' opinions for our sense of identity or worth. When we value and trust our own intuition to the opinions of others, or when we value our own inner feelings and do not transfer our authority over to others, our intuition becomes more profound, and we claim our own sacred identity.

The Law of Miracles comes into action by any person who has realised that the essence of creation is light. A master is able to employ divine knowledge of light phenomena to project instantly into perceptible manifestation the ubiquitous light atoms. The actual form of the projection, whatever it is, water into wine, medicine or a human body, is determined by the master's wish and by using powers of will and visualization. All events in our precisely adjusted universe are lawfully wrought and lawfully explicable. The so-called miraculous powers of a great master are a natural accompaniment to the exact understanding of subtle laws that operate in the inner cosmos of consciousness.

LIVING IN THE SPACE OF LIGHT

Truly understand Einstein's words *"Nothing is a miracle except in the profound sense that everything is a miracle."* Is anything more miraculous than the fact that each of us is encased in an intricately organized body, living on earth whirling through space among the stars?

My gift to shine light came to me at a very early age, and I lovingly accepted it with the great curiosity of a child and with a sense of wonder and magic. It was shown to me in a peculiar manner because of who I am and how I choose to manifest things in my life—in a playful way.

There are so many resources we can tap in to in order to become empowered human beings. We only have to ask for them to be revealed to us. We have to claim our gifts and use them. The more we use them, the more powerful we get.

The three tools to use these gifts with are intention, faith, and gratitude. Your intention must always be for the good of all of God's creation. Have faith that your gift will bring positive transformation for the good of all of God's creation—always act in the name of love. Be grateful for the gift, the opportunity to use the gift, and the outcome. Just be grateful in love.

I am a healer, and I am passionate about helping others to be healthy and full of vitality. I am gifted with healing hands. I have a holistic approach and treat the physical with the emotional, mental, and spiritual bodies, therefore am I gifted with the ability to see energy flow and blockages in and around the body. I am a good listener, therefore I am gifted with ears that can hear messages from my own body and from the bodies I treat. I work under pressures of time constraints, therefore am I gifted with the ability to see where the problem in the body arises from so no time is wasted.

All of this started with shining my light as a child and evolved to where my passion and my focus were later in life. I practised or rather played with it and believed like a child that I could do all these things. I silently clapped my hands and sang my songs of gratitude while I danced through my consulting rooms every day in an outwardly professional way.

I never stop saying thank you when I see the spark of life returning to my patients.

People often ask, "So why do you have all these gifts?" Because I said "yes!" to making a difference. I asked for the gifts. Because I see love everywhere.

Because I am passionate about what I do. Because I have fun with it. Because I have faith like a child. Because I am grateful. Because I know I Am.

I have claimed my gifts with love and gratitude, but there is so much more for me. I am passionate about nature and can just sit and stare for hours at the oceans and mountains, the plants and trees, or the stars at night. I talk to my plants when I am in the garden, and birds will stop their flight to sit close by and watch. Sometimes they call their friends to check it out too. Trees make me really happy, and I have had a few healing sessions while sitting under a tree or leaning with my body against a tree.

Once, on vacation in Tanzania, my family unexpectedly shared a bit of magic with me while we were snorkelling between uninhabited islands in the middle of the ocean. I kept falling behind because I swam without the use of flippers. My kids got hold of me and dragged me behind them, which took a lot of pressure off of me because I wasn't scared to be lost in the vast ocean. I started having fun and opened my heart to the ocean and all its fascinating creatures swimming around us. With one free hand, I made the sign of universal love to show my appreciation. I swam with my hand in front of me, showing universal love. Suddenly everything came to life! Schools of tiny fish swam in formation with us, and it felt like we were on the set of *The Little Mermaid* while Sebastian was singing "Under the Sea."

We even swam past a feeding station and had the privilege to watch without scaring them away. When we got to the boat, the swimmers were all sputtering to get their masks and snorkels off as soon as possible, asking, "What happened just now? Did you see that?"

I quietly smiled, and my daughter asked, "What was that thing you did with your hand, Mom? It was like you switched the magic on."

No words truer were spoken. We all have the ability to switch the magic on if we want to.

My life is filled with miracles because I believe in miracles, I am passionate about creating miracles, and I keep my eyes open to see the everyday miracles around me: the angel passing over my head in the clouds, the landscape turning golden at the end of the day, the weather that responds to my plea for a beautiful warm day, birds and animals that trust me and seek my company,

LIVING IN THE SPACE OF LIGHT

and the daily surprises that unfold around me if I keep my consciousness on miracles, if I am being in the moment, with an intention to see miracles arising from a space of love and gratitude, full of faith, to watch a miracle-filled world unfold. These are the moments of bliss that we can create in our lives. To create miracles in your life is so much fun and gives you an opportunity to play with life.

My daughter wanted to get married on the beach in the Western Cape in September. That time of the year can be tricky to organise a function outdoors, especially on the beach. From the beginning the two of us sat quietly together to book good weather for the occasion. It was about a year before the wedding when we had to book the venue. We gave the date and the time and said thank you for the good weather on that day, and then we left it in the hands of God. There was no doubt in our minds that there could be anything but absolutely fabulous weather on that day.

A week before the wedding, we went down to the coast to see to the final arrangements. The weather was chilly, rainy, and overcast the whole week. We saw the worried faces around us but never doubted for one minute.

Thursday was the worst day—stormy and wet. I looked up to the sky and called unto the angels. "Angels of the sky who are supposed to clear the sky for the wedding! I am sure you have everything under control, but you are making me nervous now. I think it is best if you get your air brooms out and start sweeping the sky clean now. You know it will not be a good thing to make the two of us nervous before the wedding. Thank you for doing this for me. I am so grateful."

I felt my heart filling with intense gratitude, and I knew everything would be perfect. Within a few hours, the wind calmed down a bit, and the thick clouds above allowed a ray of sunshine to peek down on us. By the afternoon it started getting warmer. I looked up at the sky and winked at the angels.

Friday morning felt much warmer, but the wind still pulled on our skirts, and there were still quite a few clouds in the sky. I was not worried anymore. We had so much to do before the big day and had to welcome the guests and see they were all settled in. Saturday morning we woke up to a clear blue sky, with a few wisps of angel-wing clouds around and no wind! I ran to my

— 77 —

daughter's room, and we danced on the lawn with bare feet to say "thank you!"

We could not have asked for better weather or better light for the photographer. Everything was absolutely perfect the whole day and evening of the wedding. We partied to the early hours of the morning on the sand dune next to the ocean. The next morning we woke up to extremely stormy and wet conditions that forced everyone to stay inside a bit longer and which gave all of us a chance to recover from the festivities of the previous day. Again, perfect!

11

SACRED SPACE

God is everywhere
God is in everything
God is in what we can see
And what is unseen
God is LOVE
Everywhere is Space
God is in that space
Sacred Space is everywhere
We have to find and activate the sacred wherever we are,
Wherever we find ourselves, and not to seek it outside of
ourselves.
The Kingdom of God is within us…and always was!

Sacred space can be as small as the breath taken in during
prayer, as large as a cathedral or as expansive as an ocean view.
Your sacred space is where you can find yourself again and
again.

—JOSEPH CAMPBELL

CAARNA

YOUR SOUL CRAVES a sanctuary from the noise, bustle and over-stimulation of the outside world. Whether it is a private oasis in a corner of your house, your garden or under a tree; your sacred space is your own personal, intimate dominion where you can re-connect and re-gather all of those deeply buried, fragmented inner parts of yourself. It is a warm, welcoming refuge where you can sit in stillness and physically express the inner workings of your mind, heart and spirit—while creatively communicating with God.

The ways we seek to enhance our lives is our constant purpose to create our own sacred spaces. For some this journey has been an unconscious affair. Life is busy and sometimes hectic, and it is easy to become overwhelmed. Even if we seek to be more connected, we may feel more disconnected from our authentic, true, spiritual selves.

Often we are unable to be with ourselves without something or someone constantly trying to distract or entertain us. We find our own life energy increasingly becomes immobilised by concerns such as co-dependency and relationship issues, weight and eating problems, addictions, anxiety, fatigue, depression, and major health crises.

Just as you could not feel something in someone else if it was not present in you, you cannot feel the sacredness of the space if the sacredness is not in you. When you have found the centre within yourself, you can live from that centre and carry it with you wherever you go.

Take the Tabernacle as an example for creating sacred space. It consists of an Outer Court, the Holy Place, and the Holy of Holies—or, more simply put: Public, Private, and Intimate space. The Holy of Holies is a place to reconnect with one's heart. These heart spaces are often overlooked in home design, yet they are essential if we want our home to feel like a refuge and retreat. We can create them for ourselves, for our children, and for our relationship with our partner, allowing ourselves to slow down a bit and remember what we hold dear. Having a Holy of Holies to share as a couple has a profound impact on the relationship. It offers a place to reconnect with your partner, where you can put aside the other roles and responsibilities that demand your focus and energy. Time spent together in a sacred space can solidify bonds of love and mutual respect and help us weather the transitions, conflicts, or challenges of daily life.

It does not matter what religion or spiritual beliefs you have, or whether you have any at all. A sacred space is something personal and meaningful to all. It can be a visual reminder for your soul's thirst for "me time" or to partake in spiritual thinking, work or practice. It is a platform for focus, where you can pray, meditate, dream, admire the beauty and sacredness of life, or just "be." It is a living, breathing, organic expression, symbolizing your spirituality, life cycles and your personal journey.

It can act as a statement to Spirit, saying: "Here I am, I acknowledge your presence and my connection with you, and I offer you this space in order to connect with you and my Higher Self in oneness and harmony. I seek refuge, truth and wisdom."

The mere act of creating a sacred space aligns us with God / Source / life force energy, for it is a creative process much like Creation itself.

It is the genesis of creating something new and meaningful for yourself that paints a colourful spiritual thread of intention and purpose through your life, a simple, sacred way to invite spiritual energies into your home and bring you closer to yourself and God on a daily level as you evolve your personal spirituality, rebirth your authentic callings and amplify your manifestation power.

Sacred space is a healing sphere that is pure, holy and safe. We can create sacred space and summon the healing power of nature anywhere on Earth. Decide what *sacred* means to you. Do you need a space for yoga, meditation, and harmony in the family or a place where you can concentrate and be creative, like your workspace? *Sacred* means uplifting, peaceful, balanced, creative, and a space where you can be fully conscious of the unlimited potential of space. Become aware that you can create sacredness in any space with your inner light—that is what it means to live in the space of light.

Dedicate a spot in your home that can become sacred. Sacred space must always have a foundation to keep the space grounded, to ensure your meditations, dreams, and prayers are grounded to earth and connected to spirit in equal measures.

Plato explicitly addressed the role of necessity in the design of the universe (so well exemplified by the five and only five Platonic solids) He wrote:

Although God did make use of the relevant auxiliary causes, it was He himself who gave their fair design to all that comes to be. That is why we must distinguish two forms of cause, the divine and the necessary. First, the divine, for which we must search in all things if we are to gain a life of happiness to the extent that our nature allows and Second the necessary, for which we must search for the sake of the divine. Our reason is that without the necessary, those other objects, about which we are serious, cannot on their own be discerned, and hence cannot be comprehended or partaken of in any other way.

The foundation is built on setting up some form of geometry that resonates with your being. It can be as simple as a triangle, a circle, a rectangle, or a square. It can be more complicated, like a tetrahedron or a cube, an octahedron or a diamond, an icosahedron, or a dodecahedron. When you enter your sacred space, the geometry will surround you to form a bubble of protection, balance, and harmony. The geometry can be as small as in the design of some fabric covering, pillow cover, or picture on display or as large as the rug covering the floor. It can be the size of a pinpoint or as large as the earth, as long as the picture in the mind can find the organised form to contract or expand in this space when you dream your dreams, say your prayers, and set your intentions for the good of all of God's creation.

Create your own altar in your sacred space. Find personal items, meaningful to you. Surround yourself with inspirational icons. Fill your space with meaningful quotes, spiritual symbols, calming music, plants and any other items that uplift your spirit. Connecting with your spiritual self opens up an amazing well to drink from when daily stresses come your way.

Once you've created your sacred space, honour it by using it with the clear intention of activating the sacredness in your space and in yourself on a regular basis. Use it to meditate for a few minutes every morning. Just sit with your eyes closed, to enjoy a few minutes of peace and quiet. Fill your heart and your space with love and gratitude.

Your ritual can be simple or complicated but, whatever you elect to do, make it meaningful to you.

LIVING IN THE SPACE OF LIGHT

A sacred space is a place to:

Get grounded
Set our intentions
Relieve stress
Recharge our batteries
Practice self-care
Affirm our worth
Claim our space
Be present
Dedicate to our purpose
Find us again and again
Bring new energy into our lives
Connect with our deeper essence
Meditate and practice mindfulness
Honour and uplift our spirit
Dialogue with our higher, deeper, and Spiritual Self
Worship God or Spirit

Whatever happens in an environment leaves an imprint. If you have meditation space, a place where you pray, a healing environment, or a location where acts of love, compassion, or worship occur, these are spaces that are quite alive and balanced.

The activities that occur in an environment can contribute greatly to the quality of the space. By the same token, environments full of death, trauma, hostility, or fear, when not balanced by positive qualities, can extract a toll on visitors and residents and alter the effect of that space on the body. Locations where there has been a painful death, accidents, traumatic exposures, or negative emotional interactions for a long time will carry the memory of those experiences in the substrate of the home or land. The clearing of those environments is an important part of re-establishing them as restorative living spaces.

The consciousness and intentions of the residents of a home or office make the biggest difference in maintaining the balance of an environment. If you bless your home, create interactions that produce appreciation, gratitude, compassion and love, you in turn place those energetic signatures on the space itself. Like our own energy systems, environments have memories and retain the imprint of the activities that occur in them.

Environments are made sacred by the people that use or inhabit them, the types of interactions that occur there, and the qualities of energy in the sites themselves. Any person that carries the intent to have balance in their lives and learns the tools to do so, attempts to create interactions with others that are respectful and caring, and treat their environment as if it were a part of their own energy system, will be creating a sacred site.

The core of home energy balancing work is the ability to create fields of vital coherent energy that have the capacity to transform and harmonize a living space into a more balanced state—to create a physical environment that interacts with the body through resonance and supports any attempts by the residents to be balanced and more vital. To harmonize an environment is to have it alive and healthy enough to support any activities we do there that create balance.

Environments are like our physical bodies—they are energy systems, have levels of consciousness ranging from the physical to the spiritual, have energy flows around, through, and within them, and can be in a state of balance or imbalance. The grid lines that run through an environment are like the meridians of our bodies, and like our own energy systems, there are centres of energy in a space that, when connected to, provide a source of balancing energy for the space.

Like our own bodies, environments are alive and continuously impacted by the energy qualities that come into it from outside sources. The vitality of a space can be affected by impinging electromagnetic fields, by earth radiations coming up from the ground underneath it, by the emissions from the materials that make up the space, and by the behaviour and attitudes of the residents. Sometimes these factors vary over time, and, like our own bodies, can be in balance one day, and out of balance the next. Like us, environments require some constant source of beneficial energy to maintain health and well-being.

LIVING IN THE SPACE OF LIGHT

As the levels of these coherent and positive energies are raised in environments, not only are the detrimental aspects corrected or neutralized, they also help keep the body in balance; strengthen the immune system; and support a higher level of consciousness, spiritual connection, and positive mental states. One's home can be nurturing, restful, alive, and a place where you can replenish your energy and connect to your own centre.

Clear this space of stagnant energies by performing a ritual of clearing. Open the windows and let some fresh air blow in to get the energy flowing. Cleansing should be repeated periodically after you begin using your sacred space. There is a clear connection between cleaning and well being. Among other things, studies have shown that a neat and clean home can actually lower Cortisol levels. Care for your home as you care for your body. As you wash, put deodorant and perfume on, and wear clean clothes every day. You must cleanse and freshen the spaces you live and work in every day. The more people who move through your space, the more tidying of your space will be necessary. Treat the spaces where you live and work like sanctuaries; treat your body, mind, and spirit like a sanctuary, and so your life will also become a space that constantly seeks balance and harmony.

When you have found the centre within yourself that is the counterpart of the sacred space, you do not have to go into the forest...You can live from that centre, even while you remain in relation to the world.

12

THE GARDEN OF STARS

NOT SO LONG ago there was a beautiful garden, where people wandered around the pathways to watch the wonders of nature play out different scenes with each visit. The garden made them calm; they could breathe easier, and they liked to spend time there.

The garden was full of flowers and scrubs and trees. There were many insects and birds visiting the garden every day. Animals were also drawn to experience the magic of the garden.

Horses came from the beginning, before the garden was even completed. It was mesmerizing to watch them as they came thundering towards the site. They stopped abruptly as they reached the outside boundaries and in front of our eyes something happened to them that no one could explain. They started entering the site one at a time, each following its own path in the geometry, while the white horse stayed outside, quietly watching them. They were all shaking and in a trancelike state. All the builders stopped working to watch them. We were probably all in a trance.

They came two more times while we were working on the layout. Each time they had a definite plan, and each time the white horse did not enter the garden. They were shaking and in a trancelike state.

The last time they came, we had just finished the layout and started construction of the water features. They came in, each one going in its own direction but staying together as a group. Then the leader walked to the centre, where we had already placed a huge rose quartz stone, and started rolling around in the dirt and dust while the others watched. He got up and stepped out of the geometry, and to our amazement the next one stepped in and rolled on the ground, got up, and left at exactly the same spot. And so they came in one after the other to roll on the ground, making sure they did not intrude on each other's experience. These horses were not trained, and all came to the farm, where the garden was, as rescue animals, but they had a plan and worked together as a team. They came again after that but never as a group and never with a display of distinctive behaviour, as before. They particularly liked to eat the colourful petals from the rose garden.

There was an abundance of rabbits and meerkats. The small buck were shy, but I managed to find them there early in the morning, just after sunrise. We did not even know there were still free roaming buck on the farm. I found a civet cat twice in the garden, and one evening he stopped to watch me as my car rolled quietly down the gravel road. He stood on the shoulder of the road and made eye contact with me as I passed a mere two metres from where he stood. I think he thanked me for the garden.

The garden was full of peacocks making lots of noise, and they seemed to multiply too quickly in number when the garden was there. They were beautiful and colourful, just like the garden.

The cows loved the garden, but they were a problem as they stampeded the garden, ate as many flowers as they could, broke the tender stems of the plants, and left dung everywhere on the pathways. They did not show respect, as the other animals did.

A camel also came, but he never entered the geometry of the garden and visited the trees that surrounded the garden. He chose all the communal meditation spots to visit. The leaves must have been sweeter to eat there.

Humans also came. They were drawn to the energy and especially to the columns of light, not visible to most eyes, that the geometry of the garden generated. Even in the early days, when the layout was in process and it looked like a bare, empty piece of land, we found ourselves standing, staring at it, totally mesmerized by some unseen force that brought a sense of peace and tranquillity to one's soul. As the garden became more developed, the light columns got taller and wider. I could see them with my eyes and feel them; some could feel them only or *see* them only. Only a few people could see and feel them. Even the ones who could not see or feel them were drawn to it. The vibration in the garden was very high, and for some it was good enough to just visit the farm to be bathed in the light.

The magnetism of the garden was an unconscious pull for most, and, as in life, we are always where we are supposed to be in the moment. The garden helped to raise the vibration of consciousness. We all vibrate at different frequencies, and when we become aware of self and what happens around self, we raise our own vibrations to become tougher and stronger in this world, like diamonds that are formed deep under the surface of the earth, withstanding conditions of intense heat and pressure to become the strongest material known to man, indestructible gems that are the highest reflectors of light.

This is a process that is achieved step by step. We are not all on the same level, but each one of us is exactly where we are supposed to be. For some it was right to pass the farm every day; others needed to visit the farm now and then. Some had to work on the farm and never set foot in the garden. Some could look at the garden but not walk the labyrinth. Some could circle the garden but not walk in the labyrinth. Some walked the labyrinth but never finished at the apex under the tree, where duality is overcome. Some could only sit under that tree but never walked the labyrinth.

I stood watching animals, birds and man from the windows of my healing centre, how they came and went and as the garden produced circular fields of energy. I watched them creating circular patterns of energy in their interaction with the garden. It was totally fascinating to see the kaleidoscope of colours that was created through this and it gave me an insight of what God sees when he looks at us every day. Beautiful mandalas of moving colours, mixing energies as we move in and out of each other's space. Forever creating works of art in the space of light.

I often think of the garden and the way the creation of it unfolded in my life. I live life in conversation with God. I am privileged that I am in a healing profession, which gives me the space of sacredness, stillness, and love to be able to talk to God all day long. If you do this six to nine hours a day, the

LIVING IN THE SPACE OF LIGHT

conversations with God wash over into the times when you are not at work. It becomes as natural as breathing. There is a certain tone or vibration when I know it is time to move *now*. I know when there is an extreme urgency.

I experienced that one morning as I arrived at my physiotherapy practice. The house I had proudly bought and renovated to accommodate the practice did not suit me anymore. I just could not fit in there anymore. It was a very uncomfortable feeling; it felt difficult to breathe.

"You have to get out into nature!" The words kept on repeating in my head, over and over again. By the end of the week, it felt like I was going to burst out of my skin.

I decided I would sell the house and look for something in nature.

The voice said, "Decide what you want for your property, and don't back down." I tested a few amounts and got a shaking head. Eventually I gave an amount that sounded ridiculous and got stillness. A good stillness. The house was put on the market, and I told the agent the price was not negotiable. She laughed. "You will never get that." I just looked at her. One week later the first offer came in for R100,000 less. I declined the offer. A few days later, another buyer came in and offered the exact amount. The house was sold at my "ridiculous" price in less than two weeks! That gave me about three months to find a new place—in nature—and to set it up as a healing centre. I definitely felt the urgency to get moving.

There was a farm called Rietvlei, just outside of town. I passed it every day on my way to and from work. Something about the place always captured my interest. The hills on the farm always felt like familiar ground, and my eyes were always drawn towards them. The location was perfect because patients just had to drive two kilometres out of town to be in nature. The farm was neglected and used as a recovery place for animals from Johannesburg zoo. It was also used to breed white lions!

My daughter Roxanne and I went there to have a look. Something strange happened. As we walked along, the animals followed us and made excited sounds. When we passed the birdcages, all the birds flew to the front of the cages and chirped. As we crossed the bridge, the geese swam next to the bridge and chatted loudly. We passed the piece of land where the white lions were kept and looked up at the large hostel at the foot of the hill that always drew my interest. The day was steaming hot as we walked up the incline towards the hostel.

Our cheeks were red and our brows sweaty when we sat down on two large tree stumps in front of the hostel. We sat there without saying a word and just breathed. I closed my eyes and saw a vision of many people gathering there, on the open veld between the hostel and the lion enclosure. More people were arriving all the time. There were columns of light reaching out into the sky where they stood. There were many angels around the crowd, and they were urging the people to step into the light. As I opened my eyes to share the vision with Roxanne, she was staring at me with big eyes. We started speaking together, and we shared exactly the same vision!

There was no question that Rietvlei Farm was where we needed to be. There were many challenges to overcome, but nothing made me stop as I forced my way forwards to secure that exact piece of ground between the hostel and the white lion enclosure.

In my conversations with God, I was given single words to use as stepping-stones on my way towards what, I was not sure. It was so intense, I felt like someone was pushing me from behind, and I often looked over my shoulder to see who was there.

First I had to create a place where many people could gather, like festive grounds. Then the word *labyrinth*. I wasn't sure what a labyrinth was and thought it meant a maze. Research taught me the difference between a maze and a labyrinth. My search showed that many people used stones to lay a labyrinth out. It sounded easy enough. I had the flat piece of land and many stones in the hills on the farm. But the words did not stop coming…

Sacred geometry. I felt clueless. Back to Google. At that time there was not much to be found about sacred geometry but enough to give me a clue that I was thinking in the wrong direction. This one kept me busy for a while. Google alone did not help. I started sharing my journey with like-minded friends Penni du Plessis and Carol de Vasconcelos. They talked to their networks, and Penni told me her friend Winks Girdwood had designed a garden using sacred geometry, and she called it the Star Garden. When I heard the name, all bells and whistles went off in my head. This was it! I phoned Winks, and she gave me a few indications that were needed on the site. While I was talking to her, I stood looking at the land, and it could not have been more perfect.

Winks came to Johannesburg with her plans for the garden, and although I did not understand a thing she explained, I knew it was what I was supposed to do and felt like I had a deeper knowledge of the project, almost like I recognised every new piece of information that was given to me.

In the two months before I had to vacate the house, we renovated the eastern wing of the hostel overlooking the site of the Star Garden as my new healing centre. During the renovations the puzzle of the Star Garden slowly but surely started forming a picture in my head.

I saw pictures of many colourful flowers. For the first time, I realised the Star Garden was supposed to be a beautiful planted garden and not just a labyrinth. It had to display the beauty of nature when man put intention and love of gardening into it.

It had to be my creation! This really scared me. I had no knowledge of sacred geometry or labyrinths, and I had no flair for gardening.

I whispered to God that I was sure He had the wrong person because apart from loving to spend time in nature, my ability to kill my potted plants until that time was embarrassing, to say the least. The messages kept coming, and I knew that God saw some quality in me that I thought was not good enough, so I trusted that anything is possible with His help.

The last command was "create columns of light." I had been shining my own light since I was a child, so I thought that one would be easy to figure out. At that time an opportunity came up to travel with my daughters. At the last minute, the destination of travel was changed, and we decided to go to Egypt. By this time I knew these things happen for a reason, and I went with the flow, knowing the visit to Egypt would solve some mystery about the proposed garden.

The pyramids and their mystical powers opened my eyes to the power of geometry. They opened my ability to see patterns of energy more clearly. I could feel the difference of different energy fields as it slowly started opening my mind to think on different dimensional levels. I stepped into a world that seemed surreal, but it was in front of my eyes to see and touch and feel. This was no movie set where fake lives were portrayed—this was real! I realised that my life up to then was small and boxed in, and it awakened a deep longing in me to find the treasures of the world.

I was called Shining One on a few occasions during the trip to Egypt. I laughed and did not really know what it meant, but the vibrations felt good. It made me feel happy, so I embraced it and let it go. On our return to South Africa, I could not wait to visit the construction site of the Star Garden. Winks and I went there early one morning. It was cold outside, and the sun was still weak in its process of rising. The energy of the garden was raw but magical. Winks stood quietly watching me as I walked along the geometry that was dug into the earth. My heart wanted to jump out of my chest, as it was filled with intense emotions of love and gratitude.

"I was given your spiritual name just now," she said when I met up with her.

"Oh, really? Please tell me!"

"Caarna," she said. "And it means the lady of the light."

I told her about being called Shining One in Egypt, and she quietly nodded her head. I thanked her and nodded my head as well. I know the light.

The columns of light were created by the geometry of the garden and strengthened by my intention and group meditations of placing two pyramids back to back, one pointing to the sky and the other pointing deep into the earth, forming a diamond or an octahedron. The effect of this turned the vibration of the garden up so much that you could feel the energy long before you even entered the farm.

The garden was my Eden where I could sit at the feet of the Lord and be taught about life and its challenges and feats. The process of creation was explained to me when I walked through the geometry and became conscious of which pathways I preferred, which were less travelled, and why I made those choices.

I was taught there is order and structure to God's creation, as it is with life. It is no haphazard business that just happens the way I want it to happen because of what I feel like at any time. There are definite rules or laws that are in place. They cannot be changed because they are the foundation that keeps the structure in place. There were many different choices you could make to walk the labyrinth, but you had to stay on the pathways, otherwise there was a chance the small plants could be damaged or you would leave footprints in the flowerbeds.

It was interesting to observe that every approach to the garden was different. Every day brought new life, and sometimes challenges were part of the package. The garden brought a sense of surrender. There were many places where I watched people letting go of their burdens. Signage boards with inspirational sayings or poems marked these spaces in the garden. It offered the opportunity to stop, breathe, fill up with positivity, surrender, and let go.

What does *surrender* really mean, and how important it is to surrender? There is an urban legend that goes:

Once upon a time, in a small village, lived an old farmer with his only son. They owned a small piece of land as well as a cow and a horse. One day his horse ran away. They went looking for their horse but to no avail. His son was distraught. The neighbours came to see the old farmer.

"God is being so harsh on you," the villagers said to console the farmer. "It's terrible what happened."

"This must be His grace too," the farmer replied calmly.

Two days later the horse returned, but not alone. Four wild steeds, fine and strong, came following. The farmer ended up with five horses all up.

"That's wonderful. You are so lucky," said the others.

"This must be His grace too," the farmer said as much gratefully as indifferently.

His son was excited though. The following day he mounted one of the wild horses to check the ride but was thrown and he broke his leg.

"These horses are no good. They have brought you bad luck," his neighbours offered their wisdom, "your son has ended up with a broken leg."

— 93 —

"This must be His grace too," the farmer replied.

A few days later, king's officials came to the village recruiting young men for the mandatory military service. They took all but farmer's son since he had a fractured leg. Out of envy and love, the villagers congratulated the farmer for his son was spared.

"This must be His grace too," he said.

Regardless of the highs or lows, thick or thin, good or bad times, when you accept everything as His divine grace, that is surrender. Surrender is another term for unshakable faith, it does not mean that only what you deem "good" will happen in your life. It means no matter what, you will continue to seek your refuge in the Divine, unconditionally.

Surrender is a way of thanking God, of loving him, of expressing yourself to him. It does not mean you do not work towards improving your circumstances, it means you accept the outcome as His grace. There is something unique about acceptance—it gives one strength and peace. The garden always helped us to find strength and peace in any situation.

It naturally worked out that there were no trees in the labyrinth part of the garden. As most of the walks took place during the day under the hot African sun, the labyrinth was sometimes uncomfortable in the heat, and to reach the point of no polarity under the oak tree felt like heaven. There was always a soft breeze, and the wide span of the branches felt like enormous outstretched wings that offered comfort and protection. There was a poem put up under the tree about creating miracles if you really believe. I saw many miracles happening under that tree in my own life as well.

My whole life had to change to take on the project of creating the Star Garden. I had to relocate my practice, become a tenant, explain my actions, deal with the frustration of not understanding and not being understood, and deal with financial difficulties because of my decision to upscale the project, to name but a few of the challenges. Despite all of this, the satisfaction and love and passion for the project will always be part of me, as it shaped me as a person and helped me to see the bigger picture.

There were many days when it became almost too difficult to deal with, but the law of rhythm taught me everything is moving to and fro, flowing in and out, swinging backwards and forwards. There is a high and a low tide.

When you are on a down swing, do not feel bad. Know the swing will change and things will get better. There are good times coming, think of them.

—Bob Proctor

"This too shall pass." I kept on repeating the words over and over, and when I looked again the challenges seemed to have fizzled out like mist in the sun.

It took blood, sweat, and tears to construct this place of healing. There was praying, dreaming, thinking, planning, meeting the right people, and going around in circles, and eventually it all came together, and the process started moving forwards. This demonstrates the Law of Vibration—everything in the Universe moves, vibrates and travels in circular patterns, the same principles of vibration in the physical world apply to our thoughts, feelings, desires and wills in the Etheric world. Each sound, thing, and even thought has its own vibrational frequency, unique unto itself.

The Law of Action must be employed in order for us to manifest things on earth. We must engage in actions that support our thoughts dreams, emotions and words. Through learning this law, we see that change is all there is. People say, "I like things just the way they are," but they are just advertising their ignorance to this important law. We must see that we are either growing or dying. Everything Is always changing. Do not resist the change.

The design of the garden, where it was supposed to be, what it needed to look like, and so on, was brought to me by visions, dreams, and strange words and concepts popping up in my mind. It felt like someone was pushing me from behind to take notice. I started listening! I was in constant conversation with God. If I asked a question during prayer or meditation, the answer or solution or the right person miraculously appeared.

Everything is made up of energy and everything has its own vibrational frequency. If you want to attract something you need to be at the same vibrational frequency as what you want—The Law of Resonance states that anything that is on the same vibrational frequency makes itself known to each other. They vibrate on the same frequency. When we send out signals on a certain frequency through as thoughts and emotions the universe respond to us with anything and everything that resonates with that frequency.

This amazing garden was designed using one central point of reference—that is, every aspect of it was connected to one central point. From that point the entire design unfolded and aligned around it. The Law of Divine Oneness states that everything is connected to everything else. This means that there is "harmony, agreement and correspondence" between the physical, mental and spiritual realms. There is no separation since everything in the Universe, including you, originates from the One Source. What we think, say, do, and believe will have a corresponding effect on others and the Universe around us. This whole project started through communication with God—my own central point of reference.

Nothing happens by chance or outside the universal laws. Every Action, including thought, has a reaction or consequence "We reap what we sow." Every one of your thoughts, words or actions sets a specific effect in motion, which will come to materialize over time. To become the master of your destiny, you must master your mind for everything in your reality is a mental creation.

When you relate something you do that you are not proficient at, to something another person does that they have mastered, you will not look good. You are using the law of relativity against yourself. Begin using this law to heighten your self-esteem. You will then become aware of how special you are in the light of truth! Whenever the law is properly used, you win. Let's remember that everyone does something better than you and, likewise, you do something better than every person you meet. At that stage I excelled at trust.

I was always rewarded with encouragement of people who also did not understand, with advice, donations of money, and features and plants for the garden. Here the Law of Compensation came into play, as blessings and

— 96 —

abundance were provided. The visible effects of our deeds are given to us in gifts, money, inheritances, friendships and blessings.

From the beginning this project evoked so much passion within me.

Every step took a lot of courage and faith. I did not understand exactly what I was doing. I had no knowledge of sacred geometry or labyrinths, and I had no flair for gardening. Despite this I kept on moving forward, going with the flow, processing what was offered to me, testing, going back to the drawing board until truth clicked in my heart. Then I knew it was right, and nothing could stop me! I was driven by passion, filled with awe and gratitude for each step that we moved forwards, and I loved every moment of it. It must have been so infectious to everyone around me because our combined efforts became one mean machine of creation and joy. As the Law of Cause and Effect states, for every action there is an equal reaction. Every cause has an effect, and every effect has a cause. Be at cause for what you desire, and you will get the effect. All thought is creative, so be careful what you wish for: you will get it. This was my garden of gratitude, and everyone felt the vibrations of love and gratitude and passion when they visited.

Everyone who used the garden experienced a raise in consciousness. They experienced heaven on earth when they wandered through the labyrinth in a meditative state. The star in the geometry was symbolic of the Law of Correspondence: "as above, so below; as below, so above; as within, so without; as without, so within."

The "above" refers to the heavens, the macrocosm, or the World Soul, while the "below" refers to the earth, the physical plane, the microcosm, or the human soul. The "without" is outer reality, "real" life, the realm in which we live, eat, pay bills, meet deadlines and interact with others. We might think of the "without" as our landscape, while the "within" would be our "dreamscape," or what Jung called our "inner world" or inner city, the realm in which we function when we dream, where we can encounter our inner partner, shadow side, ego, Self and other inner characters.

The geometry of the garden was based on the blueprint of creation, and from that piece of geometry we can draw the most intricate mandalas that will keep on unfolding around the central point. It is a reminder that we are here to create our own lives. We have free will to choose what our own works of art will look like. We have the power to change anything at any time, or we can scribble uncontrollably till the piece of art is a mess that is difficult to comprehend. It will still be your piece of art, and there will always be someone who will see method in the madness or find beauty and structure in the mess. That is why we must never despair if we find ourselves in the midst of creating messes in our lives. Sometimes we must step back a bit and look from a different angle to make sense of what we did.

There is a lesson in everything we go through or do. There is always a chance to stop and start over or to find the beauty in the experience, even if it is only to remind us not to follow that path again.

The Star Garden was the agony and ecstasy of my life. The ecstasy will always be with me. It was a sacred space given to me, and through the intention of love and gratitude, the sacredness was enhanced to become a tangible, holy space. It was easy to see and feel the sacredness of self and to communicate that to God with gratitude. It taught me to build my own sacred space within my body, mind, and spirit so I could carry it with me wherever I went. I could live from that sacred space, shine my light from within, and truly live in the space of light.

The agony was my biggest lessons in life. The ones I chose to trust, who betrayed me in the end, and the process of forgiveness over and over and over again. I also had to forgive myself for choices I made. The agony was to feel unsupported when I had a wide circle of family and friends around me and hosts of angels looking after me. The agony was being misunderstood and cursed as being a witch when I did not have the words to explain the knowing.

The Star Garden existed for only six years. Short-lived for something that was created with so much passion and love. Short-lived for something that gave so much happiness and brought so much change in people's lives.

There is a time for everything in this world. As the seasons come and go and the tide moves in and out, so things change and people come and go in the world. I would have loved it if the Star Garden could have been tended to for generations to come, but it did not happen. No matter how heart-breaking, it is what it is.

LIVING IN THE SPACE OF LIGHT

The energetic imprint of love and gratitude that was created with the garden is still there. It is clearly noticeable in the way the farm has expanded and how the school that took the healing space over is thriving. I am so grateful to know that every pupil, teacher, and parent who enters that space is bathed in blessings of love and gratitude. The farm has become a refuge for the community where people can relax and spend quality time together as families. The vision that was given to us has come to life, and it is heart-warming to know we were the pioneers of the creation of such an amazing sacred space.

Early development of The Star Garden with horses visiting

LIVING IN THE SPACE OF LIGHT

An aerial view of The Star Garden, early development

The centre of The Star Garden

LIVING IN THE SPACE OF LIGHT

The Angel of The Star Garden, not seen by the eye, showing in a picture

A wild golden wildebeest approaching me for a snack on the farm

Millions of butterflies, before the second strike of lightning on the farm

A few days after Laa La was born, with her mother Chi Chi

A day before Chi Chi's accident with Jo Jo and
baby Laa La in the background

My visit to Machu Picchu

My encounter with the eagle after the condor flew over my head

13

BAD THINGS HAPPEN TO GOOD PEOPLE

FOR A FEW decades of my life, I seemed to create abundance effortlessly. I was offered a job where my income tripled and then was offered partnership in a large, well-established practice. I worked hard, but it seemed effortless because I was so driven to be successful.

My husband and I started to make good money early on in life. We bought a bigger house and a fancier car as well as a beach house and had regular trips to the coast. We worked hard and played hard. However, none of that brought fulfilment. You can live in only one house and sleep in one bed, and the endless shopping sprees started to get boring. I used to throw the shopping bags in the back of my cupboard and forget about them. One day I cleaned my cupboard and found a stack of unopened parcels with expensive perfume, clothing, shoes, and jewellery I had bought months earlier. It really scared me. I knew I had a problem. In my mind I tried to make sense of my behaviour and take a good look at my life.

I was so driven to be a successful businesswoman and a good wife and mother that my spiritual development was put on hold for a while. I was always religious and never stopped praying and still went to church every Sunday, but my search to find my inner spiritual self was put on hold. Something inside me did not feel right, and I did not know how to fix it. It worried me, but I was so busy with work, my children, and my husband that I always put the thoughts in the back of my mind.

Until the wheels started coming off in my perfect little life. My husband was involved in a serious motorcar accident. I had two daughters, aged three years and ten months, and was pregnant with our son. I had just bought into a new practice, and my partner had decided to move to the country and left me with all the responsibilities. My husband was in hospital with a broken back and neck, and for a while we did not know if he would be OK. I had three practices to run, and life does not come to a standstill when your wheels are coming off.

Every morning I had to get up after caring for a baby and a husband. My husband had to be moved every two hours and was in so much pain that I had to help him into the shower at two o'clock in the morning. I put on my happy face and cared for more sick people during the day, just to repeat the whole cycle at night again. This carried on for the last five months of my pregnancy. By the time I was due to give birth, my husband had recovered to being fully functional and could move around without assistance. He was still in a lot of pain during the night but could help himself, although I still woke up when he started moving around.

We were in the process of renovating our home, and we were living in two bedrooms and a bathroom during the last ten weeks of my pregnancy. As usually happens with stress and trauma in a person's life, my health deteriorated when my husband became functional. At thirty-six weeks I was rushed to hospital with severe bladder and kidney infections, and I was in a delirious state for a week. I recall lying in our bedroom with all the furniture stacked up around me, listening to the radio playing next to me.

Tears for Fears sang, "Shout! Shout! Let it all out. These are the things I can do without. Come on. I'm talking to you. Come on…"

I got through the whole experience like I always do and carried my son full term. The gynae decided to induce birth on his due date, October 10, or 10/10.

Everything went well, and the pain was not nearly as severe as the previous times. I felt very much in control and calm. When the doctor decided to rupture the membranes, he said the pain would get worse and prescribed pain medication. I did not think it was necessary, so we debated the issue, and he overruled me. In those days you did as the doctor told you.

The birth was easy, and my son was absolutely beautiful and perfect. When all the excitement subsided, I started feeling disorientated and uncomfortable. I felt like grogginess was trying to sweep me away to another world. I panicked a bit and told the sister on duty how I felt.

"It's perfectly normal, my dear," she said. "Look. It is three o' clock in the morning. You need to sleep. We will keep your baby in the nursery for a few hours so you can have a nice rest." I surrendered.

As is the way in hospitals, I was woken up at seven when the staff on duty brought my son in to be fed. Something did not feel right. I felt like a zombie. My body did not feel like it belonged to me. I felt like a puppet on remote control when I got up and moved to a chair next to my bed. The sister placed my precious bundle in my arms, and my mind startled. I could not feel him in my arms, although I knew I was holding him. My mind tried to make sense of it all, and then I realised I was watching my body from above. I was having an out-of-body experience! Typical me, I sat there staring at my sleeping child with a fake smile on my face while my mind was racing to process it all.

"What is happening?" I asked myself

"You'll be OK Just give it a bit of time." The part of me looking down said

"But I can't feel him!"

"Don't worry. You are holding him."

"What if I drop him?"

Silence from up there.

"OK. We need to do something. Call the sister!"

The sister was very helpful and did not seem too concerned, which helped to calm me down. "I think you need a nice hot bath. Why don't you run to the bathroom, and I will keep an eye on him while he is still sleeping."

By this time it was even getting difficult to talk for the body sitting in the chair. I tried to explain that they needed to keep an eye on me as she helped me to get into the bath.

"Sure. You will be fine," she said with a smile, and she closed the door behind her.

I sat in that bath, trying to splash water over my body, for what felt like ages before she came to check on me. I felt myself slipping further and further

LIVING IN THE SPACE OF LIGHT

away. My slurred, inarticulate speech and laboured movements made her run out of the bathroom to get help. I can't remember much from then on.

Lots of people were coming and going while I kept on repeating, "Help my baby" over and over to make sure they got it. I recall my husband coming into the room. It lifted me a bit out of my comatose state, and I explained he had to hold our son, he needed to be loved.

As soon as I saw him holding Petrus against his chest, whispering words of love in his ear, I floated into a very dark place. At times I was vaguely aware of doctors and nurses being busy around me, but most of the time I was floating further and further away.

I saw darkness like a never-ending tunnel that sucked me in, and when I thought it was too uncomfortable to bear, I saw the most beautiful light and a place that was so familiar and so beautiful I just wanted to be there. I was home! The feeling was indescribable. Everything in my being wanted to step into that light. There was someone waiting for me on the other side. I can't recall who it was, but I was ready to leap over...when I heard my baby crying.

I froze and looked over my shoulder to see if he was OK. I know they fed him, so why was he crying so bitterly? I saw my husband was holding him, loving him, but his little face was red, and he cried tears, which newborn babies don't really do. He was terribly upset, and the only thing that could calm him down was to be held and cared for by his mother. That shocked me back to life. He was telling me he needed me in his life. I slipped back into a comatose state.

I woke up the next day feeling fit as a fiddle. When the sister walked in, I was standing at the basin, brushing my teeth. She gave a gasp, and with one step she was at my side, trying to get me back into bed. "We thought we were going to lose you," she said, "and here you are brushing your teeth! I thought I saw a ghost."

"Why?" I laughed. To me it felt like waking up from a bad dream. I remembered the out-of-body experience and not the rest where I wanted to leave this life behind. I did not realise it was the third day after the birth. I was in a euphoric state for the rest of the day. It felt so good to be in my body again. All the staff took turns to come greet me with much relief on their faces.

"You gave us such a fright," they said. When my husband came, he looked so tired, and when I asked him what had happened he pretended nothing was wrong. I got the same reaction from my doctor.

I needed to talk about it to get it out of my system, but everyone involved avoided the issue. Shock set in only the next day. I started feeling tired and very emotional. The doctor kept me in hospital for a few days longer, which was probably for the best because the renovations at home were not done yet. The contractors were still busy painting, and the fumes were not ideal for a newborn baby.

I remember very little from then on. I was in autopilot mode. I had three young children to care for, a house to decorate, and a large practice to look after. Four weeks later I went back to work for five hours a day. I was still breastfeeding. Life passed me by in a daze; even the trauma of the birth was hidden deep inside me. The danger was that everyone thought I was OK. I also thought I was OK, just emotional and listless.

When my son was three months old, I started getting sores in my mouth and on my tongue. My doctor was concerned about my health and advised me to stop breastfeeding, to give myself a chance to heal. Luckily it was time for our annual holiday at the coast. For three weeks I rested and enjoyed the fresh air and swimming in the sea. I got better physically, and by the time we got home I could deal better with daily life.

I stepped right back into all my roles—wife, mother, practice owner, therapist—and life carried on as always. Time waits for no one.

My son was a good baby who slept through at the age of two weeks. My only concern was that he cried every morning from the time I started getting ready for work till I left the house. The nanny said he calmed down after that and was perfectly good the rest of the day. This behaviour carried on for the first ten months of his life. In those days we knew very little or nothing about trauma at birth and separation anxiety or posttraumatic stress syndrome. You took what came into your life, and you dealt with it, and that was it. Tough love.

The pace of my life sped up, as the practice was growing and there was very little time to think. I was busy all the time. It was only years later that I realised what impact the near-death experience had on me and that my son was also affected by it.

Life is different after an experience like that. It has more value, and the spiritual body is awakened. I always walked close to God, for as long as I could remember, but from then onwards my conversations with God were deeper, more personal. I started questioning more, trying to make sense of this life. It felt safer to push the boundaries because I knew I could never offend God. I started the journey to find my own truth.

During that journey I was led to many different therapies to align the energy in and around my body. Some really made a difference in my life, and others made no difference. I went with my gut and stepped away from what was not my truth at that time. Unease does not always mean that something is not for you. It can simply mean you are not ready to receive it yet. Go with the flow; if it is meant to enter your life again, it will come knocking on your door.

Be aware that trauma can leave an imprint on you and affect your life. Life very rarely runs smoothly; that's just a plain fact, whether it is problems at work, financial problems, the death of a friend or family member, or some other unexpected, sudden occurrence.

Trauma is an everyday event, natural and widespread. Traumatic experiences often involve a threat to life or safety, but any situation that leaves you feeling overwhelmed and alone can be traumatic, even if it doesn't involve physical harm.

Emotional and psychological trauma can be caused by single-blow, one-time events, such as a horrible accident, a natural disaster, or a violent attack. Trauma can also stem from on going, relentless stress, such as living in a crime-ridden neighbourhood or struggling with cancer.

Not all potentially traumatic events lead to lasting emotional and psychological damage. Some people rebound quickly from even the most tragic and shocking experiences. Others are devastated by experiences that, on the surface, appear to be less upsetting.

It's not the objective facts that determine whether an event is traumatic, but your subjective emotional experience of the event. The more frightened and helpless you feel, the more likely you are to be traumatized.

People are more likely to be traumatized by a stressful experience if they're already under a heavy stress load or have recently suffered a series of losses. People are also more likely to be traumatized by a new situation if they've been traumatized before—especially if the earlier trauma occurred in childhood.

Experiencing trauma in childhood can have a severe and long-lasting effect. Children who have been traumatized see the world as a frightening and dangerous place. When childhood trauma is not resolved, this fundamental sense of fear and helplessness carries over into adulthood, setting the stage for further trauma.

These symptoms and feelings typically last from a few days to months, gradually fading as you process the trauma. Even when you're feeling better, you may be troubled from time to time by painful memories or emotions—especially in response to triggers such as an anniversary of the event or an image, sound, or situation that reminds you of the traumatic experience.

No one who has suffered a traumatic experience should be alone for any length of time. There is no shame in asking a close friend or other family member to be your confidant during this period and close friends and relatives should indeed realize this and be there for you without you having the need to ask.

It is also important to remain busy during this period of time; if you have too much time on your hands to think about your situation then this will only extend the grief and worry you are feeling. Although you might need to take a break for a couple of days or a week at the most, don't just sit about and brood during this time. Set out goals for your future looking towards the more positive aspects in life. Although at the time you might not be able to find much good it is important to remember that you won't always feel this way. So force yourself to set out goals and work towards them during hard times.

Try to keep a positive outlook and go about daily routine without changing anything. Do the same things such as shopping, cooking and cleaning,

LIVING IN THE SPACE OF LIGHT

remember to eat at regular times and take time out to be with friends. During the particular tough times remember that time does heal if you allow it to.

If months have passed and your symptoms aren't letting up, you need professional help.

Seek help for trauma when you are:

Having trouble functioning at home or work
Having aches and pains and general malaise
Suffering from severe fear, anxiety, or depression
Unable to form close, satisfying relationships
Experiencing terrifying memories, nightmares, or flashbacks
Avoiding more and more things that remind you of the trauma
Emotionally numb and disconnected from others
Using alcohol or drugs to feel better

14

ENLIGHTENING LIGHTNING

On March 3, 2010—that is, 3/3/3—I was struck by lightning. It changed my life for the better. It started off as a normal working day, and as the day started coming to an end I collected my stuff to pack into my car, which was standing under an acacia tree on the entrance corner of the Star Garden.

Typical of weather patterns in Johannesburg, the heavens opened from nowhere, and I stood watching from my window as the rain poured down. The car was parked about fifty metres from the front door, so I patiently waited for the rain to stop.

It stopped as suddenly as it had started, and I ran through the puddles to the car. I thanked Daniel, the gardener silently for paving my parking spot with stones and crystals he found on the hill behind the Star Garden. The sun was shining again, and everything looked so clean and fresh. I opened the front and back doors on the driver's side and packed all my stuff for the long weekend into the backseat. I looked at my watch and saw it was 5:55 p.m. Due to the rain, I was delayed a bit, but it was long weekend, and my family was going on a fishing trip, so there was no rush.

From nowhere an incredible bolt of lightning struck the crystal and stone paving, and I heard the sharp clicking sound, like a whip under my feet. Then came the tremendous rolling roar of thunder. In slow motion I felt something running up the back of my spine. I looked over my shoulder and saw a ball of fire on my right shoulder.

I must have lost consciousness because next I found myself half lying on the front seat with my legs hanging out of the door. I looked over to where I had been standing and saw a smoke shadow where I had stood.

My first thought was, *Oh God, now I am dead*. I started pinching my arms and legs as I recalled how lifeless my body felt when I'd had the near-death experience after my son's birth. I could feel the pinching and feel my lungs expanding and contracting. I did not feel dead. I sat for a while and looked around. Everyone had left already. I was alone on the farm.

What do you do after a traumatic experience? You pull yourself together and carry on doing what you had been busy doing. I closed the car doors and turned the ignition on. I had to get myself home. After driving four of the fifteen kilometres of the journey home, I started trembling. I did deep breathing and with an iron will proceeded home. When I arrived my teeth were clattering, as my body was shaking from head to toe. I needed assistance to get out of the car. My movements were laboured and stiff.

My husband and children were busy packing. I reassured them I was OK and urged them to finish. They sat me down in the family room and gave me something to eat and drink. I put on a brave face and acted like everything was OK. I could not eat and forced myself to drink a little. I quietly fed the dogs my food and dragged myself to my bed when no one was around.

"I just need to sleep. Tomorrow I'll be better," I kept on saying to myself as I dozed off to a place far, far away.

My family were ready to leave in the early hours of the next morning, and I managed to put a sleepy smile on when they came to my bedside to say good-bye to me. My daughter, Alicia, stayed with me, and she made no appearance, so I slept until eleven o'clock. I woke up feeling like I had just returned from the most amazing holiday. The previous day's ordeal felt like a dream, and it was difficult to even think of what had happened. I jumped out of bed feeling energised and flexible. Like a busy bee, I tidied the house and stacked everything on my workspace for what I had planned to achieve over the weekend.

The creative juices were flowing, and I even found myself moving into the zone where all creations became effortless. I felt so fabulous that there was no need to even think of the lightning. It was simply pushed to the back of my mind.

Two weeks passed, and day-by-day I felt more and more like a supercharged human being. I did not talk about the lightning because I did not think anyone would be interested, as nothing really had happened to me.

I was scheduled to do a TV interview, which was a big thing for me. I am terrified of public speaking and hate to be the central point of focus. However, on this day I was calm, and I had a wonderful interview with the very charming presenter. I saw the puzzled looks on the faces of my staff that knew me well.

"You are not scared today!" they said

"No, I'm having fun!"

End of story. Let's move on.

A few weeks later, I had a meeting with a group of friends in the Star Garden, discussing our spiritual development. While we were having tea, they all commented that I looked different. They did not know what it was, but there was something very different. I shrugged my shoulders and did not know what they saw. I told them I was feeling good and fit.

"But what happened? Why are you feeling different?" they kept on asking.

"I don't know. I just feel so energised."

Suddenly I heard this deep voice in the back of my head. " Have you really forgotten about the lightning?"

I started laughing. Remember, I am used to hearing voices in my head.

"Ah, the lightning!" I said. "I forgot to tell you about the lightning."

They sat around me as I recalled the experience for the first time. They were totally stunned.

"But how can you forget about that, and why did you not tell anyone what really happened?" they asked.

"I don't know, but I was just reminded now that it was really important and that I need to talk about it. I also need to say thank you because I am still alive to tell the story."

It reminded me how easily we can shrug things off as being insignificant even when they are life changing, as in my case. I made myself a promise to be more aware of my body, mind, and spirit and to practise mindful living, to make each moment count.

I totally enjoyed my newfound physical abilities of endurance and improved agility. So many of my fears got burnt out of existence. My fears paraded themselves in front of me, one after the other. I took the challenge and looked at each one carefully and allowed myself to live through the fear until there was nothing to fear anymore.

My physical abilities have always been a bit challenging to me. I was never a natural athlete but a rather clumsy child who still enjoyed running and playing but never excelled at sports. It did not affect my life too much, as it taught me to push my own limitations to keep up with the group. I grew up with only boys as friends, and my sister was born when I was twelve years old. The age gap was too big for us play together. As the only girl, and being a girly girl, it was accepted that I could not compete on the same physical level as the boys. It was important to be around, though, and to find my niche in the circle, like reading, writing, and creating artwork for school projects, which none of the boys enjoyed.

As you grow older, many of your physical abilities are lost because you don't use them anymore. Climbing trees and hanging from rope ladders was not part of my world anymore, but I did not want to lose what I loved most—being in nature. Our family often take hikes in the mountains, crossing streams and jumping over ravines. I like to test my physical abilities at least once a year, when I plan to do some activity that scares me a bit or one I have not done for some time. We head for the mountains to hike or go for a bicycle ride when we travel. We have enjoyed quad bike rides in the desert, snowmobile excursions, dogsledding, doing every single ride at Disneyland, swimming with dolphins and whales, taking trips to remote places in the world, and camping through Africa, to name but a few. The highlight so far has been exploring the city of Machu Picchu by foot, high up in the Andes Mountains.

I am never the most agile member of the team, but I do not care. I just do it! My children will remember me saying that to them from a very early age if they were worried they could not do something. "Just do it!" has become my motto in life. I often see disbelief in people's eyes if I tell them what I have been up to.

"You?" they ask as they secretly try to scan my body up and down to find some validation of my ability.

The first lightning helped me to stand bold in what I believed in. I challenged fear and allowed myself to feel fear and then to just do it! Two years later lightning struck again, on December 26, 2012. It was a very happy day on the farm in Nylstroom. As we got up that morning, there were thousands of white butterflies fluttering everywhere we looked. We headed off into the veld to play and take photographs of the event. The dogs had the best time ever because we played fetch with them for hours in the veld, with swarms of butterflies fluttering. It was a dreamy morning, with butterflies and soft blue skies; the wind gently played along, and even the sun stayed gentle and did not chase us to the shade of the trees.

The only thing that could get us indoors was the clouds building up to become heavy and dark in the sky. A few rumbles from afar were the deciding factor for us to head home. It started raining heavily after lunch, and it was the general consensus that it was a perfect time to take a nap.

Due to my overload of energy, I took my laptop and sat at the table on the veranda to write an article. The excitement of the morning helped me to be creative, and soon the words were flowing as everyone around me became very quiet. Raindrops hitting a tin roof can be the most soothing sound.

The sharp, cracking sound of lightning shook me as I felt electricity running through the right side of my body. This time I screamed and waited for more to happen. Nothing. Just tingling through my right leg and foot.

Everyone came running to see what had happened. I was a bit shaken, but I seemed unharmed. Everyone reprimanded me jokingly for attracting the lightning to the house. The experience was not the same as the first time, as I felt nothing afterwards, no shaking or nausea, no visible signs of trauma, as had happened the first time. My leg felt a bit funny but nothing that needed the care of a doctor.

The next day I saw a scab on my leg but thought nothing of it, as I had been working in the garden, getting very physical. The scab stayed there for weeks, but it did not worry me, so I made a point of not scratching it. Two months later the scab was still there.

We experienced a very hot weekend in Johannesburg and sat in the pool one entire day to survive the heat wave. When I got out of the pool and dried my legs, the scab came off, and I was horrified to see a hole in my leg the size of my thumbnail!

Apart from the fact that it took longer than twelve months for my leg to heal, my health started to deteriorate gradually. The supercharged human being was gone! My body started getting stiff and sore, and I got sick more frequently. Things were just not right, and I did not know how to fix it.

Three years after the second incident with lightning, someone I barely knew, named Secita, invited me to take a trip to Peru. Machu Picchu has always fascinated me, and I knew I would manage to get there someday. I did not take the invite seriously, as we had met on just two occasions before, although we felt very comfortable with each other.

Synchronicity showed me there was much more to the invite than I thought. Everything fell into place, and my husband even offered to pay for the trip. This was very unusual, as the trip was five weeks long, and we never spend so much time away from each other. From experience I knew this was one of those trips I had to take because there was work to be done.

I phoned Secita to make sure she really wanted me to join her, and of course she could not discourage me when she heard my excitement. Two weeks later my flight was booked and paid for, five months before departure. For three months the two of us did not see each other or communicate in any way. I had no idea where we were going to stay or what we were going to do in Peru for five weeks, but I felt so comfortable about everything because I knew this was bigger than me wanting to travel. I waited patiently for the voices to come, but nothing came. I still trusted the process.

Two months before departure, and after silence between the two of us, I was wondering if I needed to do my usual checklists when Secita phoned me to confirm some arrangements. A month before the trip, I felt a brief moment of concern that we may not get along, which disappeared as suddenly as it came. Two weeks before departure, we communicated briefly a few times over the phone, very chilled and relaxed.

Three week before we left, the dreams and the voices started. My husband and I were on a camping trip in Botswana at the time. I had a lot of time to be quiet and to go within with the unspoilt beauty of nature around me twenty-four hours a day.

There were no instructions or words to guide me, only questions. "What do you want? Why are you going to Peru? What is it that you need to find there? What do you want to make out of this trip? This is about you, so what do you want? What do you want? What do you want?"

The first thing that came to my thoughts was…pilgrimage. I was going on a pilgrimage to express my gratitude for the opportunity to visit the many sacred spaces in the Andes Mountains, to drink in the sacredness so it could become part of me, to infuse my body with it so I could carry it with me wherever I went.

While there are so many who do not get the opportunity to visit these, sacred places on earth, I wanted to stand in for them in prayer and positive thoughts, acting as a surrogate. I asked for guidance to show me what each daily prayer and dedication had to be about and woke up very early every morning in Peru, with a new prayer in my heart and words of gratitude spilling from my lips.

Everything about the trip and the interactions between Secita and I were effortless. We knew each other's thoughts; our needs were the same. Our souls searched for the same truth. I often had to pinch myself to make sure our Peru trip was for real.

Another planet, Peru…and so it was. From the beautiful Myburgh family from South Africa, who made Peru their home, to every shaman, guide, and driver and the staff at Casa de la Gringa, we all became beloved family. There was an amazing opening of hearts from shopkeepers, chefs, laundry keepers, and the amazing indigenous Indian tribes people who sold us their jewellery. We met other tourists who were also soul searching and ones who travelled to see the world. Each and every meeting was a celebration of love and gratitude that left permanent imprints on our hearts.

LIVING IN THE SPACE OF LIGHT

We explored the Andes Mountains by car and by foot. We climbed endless steps when we visited the ancient Inca ruins. We walked and stepped and climbed Machu Picchu with our guide, Kutcho, with small folded parcels of coca leaves in our cheeks to keep our mouths from getting dry and to provide strength and stamina I did not know I had in me to complete the journey.

Kutcho helped us to collect crystal-clear water from a fountain in Machu Picchu to take to Lake Titicaca. We delivered the water as an act of respect and gratitude towards nature. It left both Secita and me breathless as we sat alone one the deck of our boat, staring into the endless mass of water around us.

High up in the Andes, we experienced the flight of the condors. Shamans told us it is the highest honour that can be bestowed on anyone when a condor flies over your head. We were so happy to see eight condors in flight when we arrived at the site. Their flight is mesmerizing to watch, as they keep on circling and gliding in the currents of air. Their flight can pull you with them as you stand, following them with your eyes; your inner frequency can resonate with theirs, and all become one.

We spent many gratifying hours there, high up in the Andes, and my cup was flowing over. Towards the end of the day, some of our group did a hike in the canyon, hopeful to see condors. We decided to take the minibus to meet them at the end of the hike. I climbed on some boulders to stand high, overlooking the gorge down below. I was overcome with gratitude and stood exalted, thanking God for the wonders of the world and the opportunity to experience it.

An old man crossed behind me and shouted about his disappointment in not seeing one condor the whole day and even doing the challenging walk along the gorge with no luck. How was it possible, I thought, when we had seen so many?

"Maybe you will see them on your way back," I encouraged him, and he shrugged his shoulders and walked away. I took deep breaths to drink in as much of the perfect day as possible as I stood alone, with my head almost in the clouds.

I heard a commotion from down where the busses stood. People were shouting, pointing to the sky. Then I saw him! A huge condor, with an almost

— 125 —

unbelievable wingspan, flying up the canyon. As I watched him, my body started shivering. He was flying towards me! I tried to take a picture of his approach, but my hands were trembling too much. The world came to a halt around me as everyone watched the magnificent creature in his purposeful flight.

The world turned to slow motion mode as he took a dive towards me, giving his loud birdcall before he ascended above me and circled three times above my head. He then dived down into the canyon and flew back to where he had come from.

I took me a while to gather myself. I could not get my legs to walk. The world was slowly turning around me, and strange primal sounds of joy came from my mouth. Eventually I gathered my coordination back and started the walk down to the minibus. The walk was difficult because it felt like I was walking on air.

On the bus I told Secita about the experience. I could not get myself to stop shaking. It carried on for the next hour and a half to the next destination, a village in the valley with hot springs.

I had a small bite to eat to help me ground myself and felt brave enough to explore the village. As I walked down the main road, a man with an eagle on his shoulder approached me. I stopped to admire the beautiful bird, and as I reached out impulsively it effortlessly jumped onto my hand and was quite happy to sit there. It jumped onto my shoulder and allowed Secita to take pictures of us.

The trainer of the bird put his hat on my head, and the eagle flew up and sat on my head. I did a little dance of joy and got that photographed too. The eagle loved me and did not want to go back to the trainer. Eventually the trainer showed me how to hold both hands in the air in front of my head, and the eagle jumped onto my hands as I gave it a little push off to make it fly back to the trainer.

Everyone around us was cheering and thought I was very brave, but the truth is the eagle initiated the interaction, and I just received what it had to offer. All along I felt the spirit of the condor communicating with me. The encounter with the eagle was a gift from the condor to thank me.

LIVING IN THE SPACE OF LIGHT

Back at the casa, I could not wait to share my story about the incredible honour that had been bestowed on me, only to learn that a condor flying over your head is as significant as being struck by lightning. Apparently you are initiated as a natural shaman when struck by lightning three times or when being honoured by the condor.

Nonchalantly I told our guide that I had been struck by lightning twice and then had the condor flying over my head.

"Oh, but that means you were initiated as a shaman!" they cried out.

I smiled and thought, *I am a natural healer. I have always been one.*

15

To Breathe Is to Live

WHEN HUMAN BEINGS, along with mammals, birds and reptiles, are born they take their first breath—and with their last breath, life withdraws from the body. Breath affirms relationship with the world. In order to maintain life we must draw in the oxygen needed from the atmosphere and we must release carbon dioxide into that atmosphere.

The air we breathe is composed primarily of nitrogen gas and oxygen gas with a small amount of other gases, including carbon dioxide. All of these individual molecules are constantly rearranged and recycled through biochemical and geochemical processes. The individual atoms making up those molecules, however, have been on earth for a long time—very little carbon, oxygen or nitrogen is lost to outer space, and only the occasional meteor brings a small extra-terrestrial source of new carbon or oxygen to this planet. So, every breath you take and every bite you swallow is composed of atoms that have been here for a long time.

It's certainly possible to imagine a scenario where you breathe in a molecule of oxygen gas and, in one of your billions of cells, it gets combined with carbon from last night's dessert to make carbon dioxide. Your exhaled molecule of carbon dioxide is taken up by a young oak tree and, with the help of sunlight, the carbon gets converted into a molecule of cellulose that gets locked into that tree's biomass for years. Eventually, over hundreds of years, that tree will grow, die and decompose. As it decomposes, that atom of carbon

— 128 —

LIVING IN THE SPACE OF LIGHT

is released back to the atmosphere as carbon dioxide and is used to generate oxygen through photosynthesis.

That newly formed molecule of oxygen might be available to your great-great grandchild. It's not the same molecule of oxygen that you breathed in years before, but it could be traced back to atoms that once passed through your body. In fact, this concept is also true of the food we eat. There may have been a carbon atom in last night's dessert that was once integral to the structure of Julius Caesar's bone tissue.

Prana, or life force, is energy, vitality, and power. Prana is received from the sun, from our food, and from rest, but the most important source is through breathing. Prana is the foundation and essence of all life; the energy and vitality that permeates the entire Universe. Prana flows in everything that exists. Prana itself is totally pure and neutral, just as the spring-water of a river is clear and clean. In its course, the river picks up many substances, which change the quality of the water. Exactly the same occurs with Prana. Prana flows into the body clean and pure, but how it departs depends upon the individual—on their lifestyle, their inner qualities and feelings, the type of food consumed and the environment and company in which one lives. The quality of the Prana that radiates from people impacts both the surrounding environment and the individuals themselves.

It is thought that the quality and quantity of the prana has a direct relationship to the state of mind. Due to the stress of planetary conditions for many people, the flow of prana has been disrupted, resulting in conditions such as fear, worry, depression, doubt, and many other negative emotions that often lead to physical illness.

We all share this same breath—the animals, the plants, and our fellow human beings. Simply holding this recognition in mind as we breathe in and out can be a simple spiritual practice that, over time, serves to foster the consciousness of oneness.

The ancient masters of Yoga believed that the manner by which one breathes determined the length and quality of life, a view based on the observation of the rhythms of nature. It was thought that all living things possessed a certain number of breaths and the idea developed that slow, rhythmic breathing, by keeping the body well supplied with oxygen, and contributed to a longer and more harmonious life. One single exhale can extend out into the spaciousness of all that is around you. The next inhale can allow that vast amount of space to enter into your body and awareness creating a sacred place to rest in and be nourished from.

There are more molecules of water in a cup of water than cups of water in all the world's oceans. This means that some molecules in every cup of water you drink passed through the kidneys of Genghis Khan, Napoleon, Abe Lincoln or any other historical person of your choosing. The same goes for air. There are more molecules of air in a single breath of air than there are breaths of air in Earth's entire atmosphere. Therefore, some molecules of air you inhale passed through the lungs of Billy the Kid, Joan of Arc, Beethoven, Socrates or any other historical person of your choosing.

You know that our breathing is the inhaling and exhaling of air with the lungs that lie round the heart. The air passing through the lungs envelops the heart. Thus breathing is a natural way to the heart. Collect your mind within you, lead it into the channel of breathing through which air reaches the heart and, together with this inhaled air, force your mind to descend into the heart and to remain there.

The cycle of the breath governs all life and as we pattern our lives thereby we become more effective. We breathe more deeply and easily. Life begins to flow without so many struggles as we have faith in the soul's wisdom and its ability to establish relationships. It takes time and patience to establish these new rhythms that so often seem to run counter to much of contemporary culture.

As one masters the breath, one masters life. The most effective way to do such difficult things as climbing a mountain and giving birth to a child is through the rhythmic breathing that enables the consciousness to transcend physical and mental constraints by focusing on something that links into the universal current that gives strength and a certain transcendental quality.

Due to the stress of contemporary life many people breathe in a shallow, disjointed manner, often with little conscious recognition that this is so. In our race to do, we forget to breathe. People are often out of touch with the effects

LIVING IN THE SPACE OF LIGHT

that stress is having on them unless they begin to breakdown physically. There is a widespread condition today wherein the prana is short-circuited, creating blockages in the flow of energy with a consequent depletion.

A type of "breath apnea" that occurs when people use too much technology. We forget to breathe and we need to bring back this focus. This situation is particularly damaging for young children who increasingly don't want to go out to play. Children's sensitive natures become easily over stimulated and this addiction to technology causes actual changes within brain chemistry.

All physical and mental power comes from the flow of energy around your body. Energy is lost when you are tense or stressed. Centering redirects negative energy in a beneficial way. Use centering to improve your focus and manage stress whenever you need to keep a clear head in difficult circumstances, to channel your nerves so that you can communicate clearly, compassionately and effectively.

The process starts by becoming aware of your breath. Breathe

Find Your Centre or "physical centre of gravity" It is visualized as being about two inches below your belly button. Direct your breath to your centre or breathe into your centre and exhale out of your centre.

Redirect your energy into achieving your goal or breathe into your intention of what you wish to achieve.

He who half breathes half lives.

—ANCIENT PROVERB

Breathing is unquestionably the single most important thing you do in your life. Breathing right is the single most important thing you can do to improve your life.

—SHELDON SAUL HENDLER, MD, PhD

Breath is the key to our biology as well as our spiritual nature. Without it, we do not survive; with it, we thrive. A deep, full breath provides us with incredible amounts of energy, vitality and clarity; a shallow breath pattern promotes disease, accelerates the ageing process and becomes the greatest contributor for low energy. Every one of the body's systems, from detoxification to burning fat to moving lymph, requires oxygen.

A consistent, shallow breath means the body doesn't have enough fuel to eliminate toxins and fats so it stores them.

Most of us are not taught to breathe, yet when we are shown how to fully use our complete respiratory system we bring health to parts of our body that have become stagnant from years of shallow breathing. Deep breathing uses the diaphragm, which stimulates a gentle massage of the abdominal organs. Without this vital massage common ailments arise such as a sluggish digestive track/ colon, tension in the lower back, stagnation in the reproductive organs and more.

Virtually every health condition and human activity is improved with optimal breathing. Clinical studies prove that oxygen, wellness, and life span are totally dependent on proper breathing.

When people refer to being grounded, it means the extent to which your soul and your energy are connected with the Earth and the energy of the Earth. This is what it means to be rooted firmly in the Earth. As much as it's important to keep an open channel with the divine to allow for divine energy to flow down from the Spiritual Realm, it's equally as important, if not more so, to keep an open channel with the Earth, allowing energy to flow up from the Earth.

All organisms and objects existing on the physical plane of Earth not only receive their energy from the Earth, but also deposit their energy back into the Earth. Just as the Divine energy flows to us from above, the Earth energy flows up to us from below. The energy in your aura consists of the energy from your soul, the energy from the Earth, and the energy from the Divine. As a physical and spiritual being, you receive energy from within yourself, and both realms to stay balanced, centred, and healthy.

Do you notice you feel better when you walk barefoot on the Earth? Recent research has explained why this happens. Your immune system functions optimally when your body has an adequate supply of electrons, which

LIVING IN THE SPACE OF LIGHT

are easily and naturally obtained by barefoot contact with the Earth. Research indicates that electrons from the Earth have antioxidant effects that can protect your body from inflammation and its many well-documented health consequences. For most of our evolutionary history, humans have had continuous contact with the Earth. It is only recently that substances such as asphalt, wood, rugs, and plastics have separated us from this contact.

It is known that the Earth maintains a negative electrical potential on its surface. When you are in direct contact with the ground (walking, sitting, or laying down on the earth's surface) the earth's electrons are conducted to your body, bringing it to the same electrical potential as the earth. Living in direct contact with the earth grounds your body, inducing favourable physiological and electrophysiological changes that promote optimum health. The Earth is a natural source of electrons and subtle electrical fields, which are essential for proper functioning of immune systems, circulation, synchronization of biorhythms and other physiological processes and may actually be the most effective, essential, least expensive, and easiest to attain antioxidant.

Modern science has thoroughly documented the connection between inflammation and all of the chronic diseases, including the diseases of ageing and the ageing process. It is important to understand that inflammation is a condition that can be reduced or prevented by grounding your body to the Earth, the way virtually all of your ancestors have done for hundreds if not thousands of generations.

To visualise grounding happening, simply place your feet on the ground, hip width apart, imagine energy coming up through your right foot, travelling up your right leg, your thigh, your hip, your stomach, your chest, and through your throat to your crown. Then imagine this energy flowing back down through the crown, following the left side of the body, until it exits through the left foot, back into the Earth.

Everyone can benefit from taking a moment to focus on him or her and his or her connection with the Earth—and you don't even have to be outside to do it! You'll find that in grounding yourself, you'll feel calmer, more relaxed, and more put together. And with practice, you'll need less than 5 minutes a day to ground yourself, replenish your energy, and restore your connection to the Earth.

Learning to ground your energy is very easy, and once you practice it a few times, you'll be able to ground yourself quickly and effectively on a daily basis. Since grounding and becoming rooted with the Earth is so relaxing, and takes very little time, it may be something that you decide to do as a meditation—in small bursts, multiple times a day. When you're first learning how to ground, try to find a place where you will be undisturbed for the duration of the meditation.

Take a few deep breaths, slowly inhaling and exhaling, noticing your lungs filling up with air and your stomach expanding with each inhale. Fully exhale, noticing your stomach shrinking and your lungs completely emptying. As you do this, take note of any anxiety or worry that is already slipping away, simply by this action. Imagine yourself breathing in white light the divine, and exhaling worries, thoughts, or anxieties that may be visualized as grey smoke. Inhale white loving energy and exhale grey smoke. Release. Continue this exercise until you feel intuitively ready to move on.

Begin to imagine yourself strongly anchored to the ground. Start to focus your energy downward, visualise the energy in your body flowing downward to the Earth, out through your feet. Imagine your body as a tree trunk that extends down from your feet, through the floor of your house, through the basement, through the foundation of the house, and finally breaking through the Earth. Continue to imagine this tree trunk traveling down through the Earth, imagine its roots breaking through layers and layers of bedrock, until your trunk finally reaches the centre of the Earth.

Once you've reached the centre of the Earth, take note of what this looks like to you. Is it flowing with magma? Does it look like a crystal cave? Is it filled with white light? The energy stored at the centre of the Earth is the one of the most powerful, purest forms of healing, cleansing and restoring energy. Imagine the roots of your trunk circling around the healing and restoring Earth centre, hugging the core, draping over it. Imagine this energy as a strong, electric white current of restoring energy, and follow it as it pulses and flows back up your tree trunk.

LIVING IN THE SPACE OF LIGHT

With each inhale, watch and consciously feel as that healing energy flows up your tree trunk, through the layers of bedrock, through the sediment, through the foundation of your house and finally through the floor beneath your feet. Feel as that energy reaches your feet and flows into your physical body. Continue to follow that energy as it completes its loop through the body, entering through your right foot, flowing up the right side of the body, to the top of your head, crossing over to the left side of your body, flowing down the left side and exiting back into the Earth through the sole of your left foot.

The more you give the weight of your lower body into the earth the more gravity will create an upward lift through your entire torso. Think feet, legs, find some nature, eat, take regular breathing breaks, breathe into your heels, stay hydrated, remember you have a body, massage your feet, jump up and down, squat, exercise, go for a walk, spend time in nature, walk away from technology, hug a tree, look at the clouds, sky, sun and moon, feel the air.

16

TO BE IN TOUCH

TOUCH IS THE first sense to develop in the womb and the last sense to leave in old age. It is essential to the health and well being of human's emotional, physical and mental development.

Touch is the language of body awareness. We experience life through our senses.

The sight of a loved one will touch the heart.

The sound of beautiful music will touch the soul.

The smell and taste of homemade cooking will touch childhood memory.

A loving hug will touch the ability to cope with life and love.

The hands are sensitive instruments of communication. A simple touch will convey thoughts or desires that are in the mind; the receiver will interpret these on a physical level and sense the intention behind the touch.

Touch is the first language we learn and the only truly universal communication that humans share. It wakes up the prefrontal areas of our brain, which control our ability to relax and emote. A touch to the shoulder sends a message to the brain more powerful than words of support. Holding someone creates a surge of oxytocin, a hormone that helps create a sensation of trust and reduces levels of the stress hormone cortisol. Touch tells us there is someone at our backs to share the load—one of the primary impetuses for human relationships.

LIVING IN THE SPACE OF LIGHT

Every human being needs to touch and be touched. Each of us has thoughts and feelings so deep and personal that words will simply not bear their weight. Yet, we long to communicate them, to share them with another. Our most intense joy is amplified and given permanence by being shared. Our deepest fears and anxieties are made endurable and manageable by being shared. But they can only be truly shared in their full depth and significance when they are shared in the totality of who we are.

In today's world, technology has reduced the amount of physical contact that people have with each other on a daily basis. With automatic bank machines, online shopping, internet, email and voice mail people can make appointments, dates or decisions without ever actually talking to or seeing another person.

Our Western culture has achieved such a level of worship of intellect and intellectualising that we are terrified of touch. Touch is almost a forgotten language in the larger part of our contemporary world. In many people's minds, it has become synonymous with sex. This is a sign of a sexually "uneasy" and "out of touch" society. Everyday activities are carried out in a mechanical way, with no real physical awareness. Only when there is pain or disease do we become aware of our life in the body.

The psychological impact of touch goes beyond physical and mental health. Researchers have shown that touch is a powerful persuasive force. Studies have shown that touch can have a big impact in marketing and sales. Salespeople often use touch to establish a camaraderie and friendship that can result in better sales. In general, people are more likely to respond positively to a request if it is accompanied by a slight touch on the arm or hand.

The need to touch can be expressed in overt hostility.

It is seen in participation and watching of contact sports.

It is seen in the disciplining of children.

It is seen in the various outbursts of physical violence.

It is seen in much anti-social behaviour.

The expression of strong hostility keeps the other feelings from being revealed. There is more love present, but hidden, in most of our acts of anger than we are often aware of. Tragically, many a child is only able to get physical intimacy from parents by misbehaving.

CAARNA

The benefits of touch to a person's health are phenomenal:

- Touch can reassure, relax and comfort.
- Touch reduces rapid and irregular heartbeats (arrhythmias)
- Touch reduces depression, anxiety, stress and physical pain
- Touch increases the number of immune cells in the body
- Touch improves immune function
- Touch can reduce pain
- Touch can improve pulmonary function
- Touch stimulates growth in infants
- Touch can lower blood glucose
- Touch has powerful effects on behaviour and moods.

There is some evidence that the level of aggression and violence among children is related to lack of touching. Touch is vital to the positive health and development of all human beings, regardless of age. Humans need to touch and be touched, just like they need food and water. It is a way of communicating, lifting their spirits, and experiencing happiness in their lives. Without it they experience sadness, loneliness and isolation.

People have lost touch with the wisdom of the body. This wisdom is accessed through love and reverence for the miracle of life in this physical form. Pleasure, ecstasy, bliss, orgasm, natural instinctual intelligence, the thinking process (mind), intuition, inner knowing (gut feeling), wisdom, feelings (physical or emotional), and love are but a few of the qualities that can manifest only through our bodies. They bring an essential contribution to the meaning of life.

"When you begin to touch your heart or let your heart be touched, you begin to discover that it's bottomless, that it doesn't have any resolution, that this heart is huge, vast, and limitless. You begin to discover how much warmth and gentleness is there, as well as how much space."

—Pema Chodron

LIVING IN THE SPACE OF LIGHT

Illness and unrest are your body's way of communicating what needs attention, and maybe you've ignored the symptoms because you didn't recognise them for what they are—messages or warnings.

Your body is programmed for survival. Heeding early warnings protects your health. Familiarise yourself with how your body speaks to you. It wants you to be well. It will tell you if you are not.

How we feel = our body's way of communicating

Hippocrates wrote over two thousand years ago, "There is a measure of conscious thought throughout the body. This is practical wisdom you can live by."

Our body's messages start at a quiet whisper, get louder, and escalate when you just won't listen and eventually the body can no longer cope.

Sight, sound and touch are all interpretations of your sense organs decoding the vibrations of different frequencies around. Your eyes create images by decoding the vibrations around you; you ears create sound by decoding the vibrations around you; and your body as a whole feels touch by interpreting vibrations around you. The human body is designed with sense organs that have the capacity to interpret vibrations—all your sense organs are just receptors that can decode vibrations around you and thus create the perception of reality. Your body as a whole is also just energy vibrating as different cells, and the thoughts you think are also forms of energy vibrating at particular frequencies.

Some senses are obvious: everyone knows about vision, hearing, smell, balance, taste, touch, temperature and pain. There are more. Chemical information from the outside world has always been important to living creatures. A fascinating array of chemical sensors and processors exist in the living world.

Vision, hearing and smell are distance senses that inform about events far away. Sensors on the surface of the body inform about close contacts. Light touch, pressure, temperature, vibration, itch and pain are sensed by skin receptors. Movement sensors in the inner ear tell us about our orientation in space and the effects of gravity. Sensors in muscles and joints inform about our movement in space-time and provide information about contact with the ground. Inner sensors are providing information to the brain about conditions in the body and feedback information the brain about the consequences of actions taken.

Inner senses belong to two groups—the most ancient chemical kind and a more modern and rapid electronic kind. The digestive tract for example is supplied with dense innervation, an internal Internet that provides electronic networking. Neural communications are sent to and from the brain via the autonomic nervous system. The dialectic of approach/avoidance is expressed in the two divisions of the autonomic nervous system; the parasympathetic network corresponds to eating, rest and pleasure; the sympathetic system corresponds to action, fight and flight.

Chemical messages are broadcast both ways by substances secreted into the blood. These circulating messages tend to have whole body effects. There are several classes of chemical messengers: hormones, peptides, neurotransmitters and cytokines (produced by immune cells).

Getting out of your head and into your body is an empowering habit. Your body's intelligence constantly sends you physical messages. These messages can come in the form of tightness, tingling, heaviness, or some indescribable feeling known only to you. Tuning into these messages will tell you more about your posture, stress, emotional state, fears, state of health, joy, happiness, and an overall state of balance.

Here are some ways we describe how these energies feel to us that might help you increase your awareness of them:

- Buzzing or tingling, like when your leg is sleeping
- Prickly, like static electricity
- A feeling of heat without a heat source
- A feeling of cold without a physical source
- A sense of a rising or falling pitches without any audible sound
- A feeling of something flowing through you like wind or a stream or current of warm water
- A feeling like a wave passing through you
- Pressure or a pushing sensation with nothing touching you

LIVING IN THE SPACE OF LIGHT

- A pulsing sensation that is not in time with your heartbeat
- A sensation of bubbles rising like in carbonated water
- A clanging sensation, like striking a piece of metal held in your hand with a hammer
- A spinning or spiralling sensation
- A fluttering or shimmering sensation
- A sensation like a change in altitude or barometric pressure
- A sense of lightness that wasn't present before
- A sense of expansion in some way
- A shift in consciousness, like meditation or falling asleep
- A sudden sigh or yawn

It's vital to re-train yourself to override mechanisms you've developed to push through discomfort. To prevent illness pay special attention to physical distress signals. Honour your body's messages; don't discount them.

Simple, prompt action is sometimes all it takes. If you're tired, rest. If you're hungry, eat a delicious meal. If you're stressed, get a relaxing massage. The price of not listening? You could come down with the flu or maybe your back goes out. If you still don't listen there may be chest pains, ulcers, depression. The thermostat gets turned up until you pay attention.

While I was busy writing this book, I often felt despondent because my busy lifestyle interfered with the process. I often wished I could take time out to focus on my writing. Out of the blue, I developed cellulitis in my right leg. I ignored it till I got so sick, I could hardly lift my head off of the pillow. Only then did I visit a doctor. He immediately ordered strict bed rest. I had never been off of work for longer than three days. It was like being sentenced to jail. I decided to take the opportunity to write during the downtime. One week became two weeks, and eventually I landed in hospital for surgery. I was amazed how much I achieved during that time but could not wait to get back to work.

I did not ease myself back into the process but just jumped back into the old ways of doing. Two weeks later I found a sensitive spot on the inside of my left ankle. My good leg! I thought it was a bruise I had received while we were on our farm. I ignored the pain, as it was not nearly as painful as the right leg had been. A week later I knew there was something seriously wrong. The pain kept me awake at night.

When the bruise started forming an angry-looking lump, I asked my daughter to have a look, and she found four spider bite marks on my leg. Eventually I consulted a doctor. By that time I had an abscess, which burst and left a huge hole in my leg. The doctor scolded me for being irresponsible and urged me to take better care of myself.

I was in a state of shock when I saw what it looked like. I couldn't believe something like that could happen to me! I realised there was a lesson in this for me.

"Please, God, show me what I have to learn from this, so I can just move on with life!" I said.

I realised I do not practise what I preach about body awareness. I did not take good care of myself. I did not feel I deserve time out to rest for full recovery. I ignored the subtle messages and needed a harder push, which almost cost me my leg, before I learned the lesson!

I once again knew how important good health is and thanked God for blessing me with it. I could not go through more with my legs and decided there and then that I had to heal—there was no other way!

I forgave myself for not taking good care of me and started doing all the healing practices I use on others on my own body—the violet flame, the diamond grid, lots of breathing, and constant prayer. There was so much support for me from friends and family who prayed for me. Within five days the huge gaping hole in my leg had closed. I did not need a skin graft or any other surgical intervention. The doctor was stunned, and no one who had seen the wound could believe it healed so fast.

This experience showed me how powerful these tools are if we embrace the knowledge, practise it with unyielding faith, and trust that God will take care of it. That is the truth, and I had first-hand experience of it.

17

THE PATH OF LEAST RESISTANCE

Life is a series of natural and spontaneous changes. Don't resist them—that only creates sorrow. Let reality be reality. Let things flow naturally forward in whatever way they like.

—LAO-TZU

No MATTER HOW much structure we create in our lives, no matter how many good habits we build, there will always be things that we cannot control and if we let them, these things can be a huge source of anger, frustration and stress. Modern life is full of hassles, deadlines, frustrations, and demands. For many people, stress is so commonplace that it has become a way of life. When you are constantly running on emergency mode, your mind and body pay the price.

Stress symptoms may be affecting your health, even though you might not realize it. You may think illness is to blame for that nagging headache, your frequent insomnia or your decreased productivity but stress may actually be the culprit. Being able to recognize common stress symptoms can give you a jump on managing them. Stress that's left unchecked can contribute to health problems, such as high blood pressure, heart disease, obesity and diabetes.

The simple solution is to learn to go with the flow. Smile, breathe, and go slowly.

What is going with the flow? It's rolling with the punches. It's accepting change without getting angry or frustrated. It's taking what life gives you, rather than trying to mould life to be exactly as you want it to be.

Realize that you can't control everything. We don't control the universe, and yet we seem to wish we could. All the wishful thinking won't make it so. You can't even control everything within your own little sphere of influence—you can influence things, but many things are simply out of your control.

*Become aware. You can't change things in your head if you're not aware of them. You have to become an observer of your thoughts, a self-examiner.

Be aware that you're becoming upset, so that you can do something about it.

*Breathe. When you feel yourself getting angry or frustrated, take a deep breath. Take a few. This will allow you to calm down.

*Get perspective. When you get angry over something happening—the car breaks down, the kids ruin the microwave—take a deep breath, and take a step back, like when you're watching a movie and the camera zooms away and you can see much more of the world on the screen than you could before. Then whatever happened doesn't seem so important. A week from now, a year from now, this little incident won't matter. No one will care, not even you. So why get upset about it? Just let it go, and soon it won't be a big deal.

*Practice. It's important to realize that, just like when you learn any skill, you probably won't be good at this at first. Skills come with practice.

*Baby steps. Along the same lines, take things in small steps. Don't try to bite off huge chunks—just bite off something small at first. Make your first attempts to go with the flow small ones.

*Laugh. It helps me to see things as funny, rather than frustrating. That requires a certain amount of detachment—you can laugh at the situation if you're above it, but not within it. Try laughing even if you don't think it's funny—it will most likely become funny.

LIVING IN THE SPACE OF LIGHT

*Realize that you cannot control others. We get frustrated with other people because they don't act the way we want them to act. We have to realize that they are acting according to their personality, according to what they feel is right, and they are not going to do what we want all of the time. Accept them for who they are and accept the things they do.

*Accept change and imperfection. When we get things the way we like them, we usually don't want them to change. But they will change. It's a fact of life. Instead of wanting things to be "perfect" (what is perfect anyway?), we should accept that it could never be perfect to suit everyone in this world.

"Ring the bells that can still ring. Forget your perfect offering. There's a crack in everything, that's how the light gets in"

LEONARD COHEN

Enjoy life as a flow of change, chaos and beauty. Try seeing the world as perfect the way it is. It's messy, chaotic, painful, sad, dirty...and completely perfect. The world is beautiful, just as it is. Life is not something static, but a flow of change, never staying the same, always getting messier and more chaotic, always beautiful.

18

FEAR = SELF-INDUCED SUFFERING

WE LIVE IN an ever-changing world; in fact change is the only constant. One thing you can be sure of is that things will change! We don't always like change because it pulls us out of our comfort zone. It is exactly at this point—at the end of the comfort zone—that life begins.

We need flexibility to steer us through an ever-changing landscape. Like the saying goes, *things start moving when you start moving.*

Flexibility starts in the body. A body that moves strengthens the physical vehicle. A moving body keeps the mind going. An active mind is needed to find your truth. A moving body helps to shift emotional debris. Balanced emotions enable us to see not only with the eyes, to hear not only with the ears, to smell not only with the nose, to taste not only with the tongue, and to touch not only with the hands.

Learn to go with the flow. Take the path of least resistance. If the currents of life get too strong and you lose control, relax—find your safe space, centre and ground, don't ever forget to breathe, and let go to allow life to take you where you are supposed to be.

While you are in the strong pull of the churning waters around you, find something strong to hold on to—faith—and enjoy the ride. Fear will only take the pleasure out of the experience, and it spends far too much of your valuable physical energy. Save that energy for when you reach steadier ground and you have to pull yourself from the debris to walk on firm ground again.

LIVING IN THE SPACE OF LIGHT

You cannot control everything that happens in your life, but you can control how you choose to react to what happens. You cannot control how another person chooses to experience life or react to what happened in life. Be concerned about your own experience, and become the observer to the experiences of others. Let go of fear; take control of your own life.

Most of us allow fear to control us. It can paralyse us, keep us locked in desperate situations, and stop us from living the lives of our dreams.

We are human beings in a world of constant change. This is scary. We are afraid we won't be OK in the chaos of change, that we will fail, that we will be judged, that life won't turn out OK. We see fear as an enemy to be defeated, or it will defeat us.

Fear is a part of us, and therefore we should not try to "destroy" it. It can't be destroyed, because while we can dissipate one particular fear in one particular moment, we will still have fears after that. Throughout our lives we will have encounters with fear. It's not something that can be eradicated—it's a basic part of life. Get to know the compulsive and addictive activities that can keep us stuck in a place of fear and how they all come from stories that play through the head every day.

Facing fear does not mean we have to start bungee jumping, purposely trap ourselves in elevators, or allow tarantulas to climb all over our bodies. Feel fear in your body as physical discomfort or a sense of unease as we watch the fear arise, and observe it in the mind, from a distance.

Because I live life in a playful way, Disneyland helped me to burn away many of my fears, without even realising it. My first visit to the happiest place on earth was when I was in my twenties, and I remember doing only a few rides—not because of the long queues but because of fear. My second visit was in my fifties, with my daughters and cousins. We had the best time ever! Something in me drove me to do every single ride, no matter how much fear it evoked in me. I did not try to make so many excuses, and if I tried, the girls just laughed and pushed ahead. I did not tell them I was scared, especially when I looked around and saw many people much older than me having so much fun. It made me realise most people in the queue must have felt fears or doubts that they could do it, but they just did it!

— 147 —

And were those not the words I always used to urge my kids along if they had to do something they did not enjoy or something that felt difficult or impossible to do? "Just do it!"

I kept on repeating those words over and over to myself at Disneyland from one ride to the next. I did not even know it helped me to burn away many of my other fears as well. Whenever I need encouragement, or if I need to stop procrastinating, those words automatically come into my head, and because of the Disneyland connection the thought is happy and attached to a sense of achievement.

Take that leap of faith, and just do it!

The greater part of human pain is unnecessary. It is self-created
as long as the unobserved mind runs your life.

—ECKHART TOLLE

Accept the fear. Do not feel bad about it, don't try to crush it, and do not wish it weren't there. It's a part of you. It's a part of life. Accept it.

Feel how the fear is hurting, and see it is self-caused.

Let go of the suffering by letting go of the fear.

Think rationally about the fear, give it a little space, and consider it. What's the worst-case scenario? Would you basically be OK? The answer is almost invariably yes—maybe life wouldn't meet your "ideal," but you will always find a way out and be OK in the end.

Be grateful for who we are and what life actually is as opposed to what it's not, or what we're not. Appreciate ourselves, and others, and life at this moment.

This is a process of awareness, acceptance, seeing the pain, finding gratitude, and being in the moment. While we can't stop our minds completely, we can take control over them and create moments of peace for ourselves. The second, when thoughts or fear arise, try to do the following as soon as you are aware of what's taking place in your mind and body:

Stop.

LIVING IN THE SPACE OF LIGHT

Take a long, deep breath in and out. In your mind say "IN" as you breathe in and "OUT" as you breathe out in order to ground yourself in the present moment.

Feel the ground beneath your feet. Notice the way your clothes feel against your skin, the wind against your face, and the sun on your cheeks. Listen to the birds singing, the rain falling around you, or the ticking of a nearby clock.

All this will ground you in the present moment. Even if thoughts want to drag you away with them, coming back to recognize the breath will give you the control you need to prevent this from happening.

Follow these steps until you feel that the thought or storyline in your mind has moved on, or until you feel that the pull of your thought or fear has dissipated slightly.

You can also replace your fears and negative thoughts by singing a happy song in your mind or out loud as soon as you are aware of fear entering your mind. Eventually the song will come to mind whenever there are triggers that usually set the fear in action.

At this point, you can return to whatever you were doing, and hopefully you will have prevented yourself from suffering in that moment.

Unfortunately, these steps are by no means a quick fix in saving you from the suffering we all encounter every day. In fact, at first it will take all your energy and resolve not to react to what your mind and ego are doing.

It's also quite possible that even once you've covered these steps, you will still get lost in your thoughts and fears by comparing yourself to others. Whether you do this or not isn't the point. The point is that you've finally managed to sit back and look at your thoughts and fears. Once you have done this, you've begun the process of taking control of your mind and your life.

The only thing we have to fear is fear itself.

—FRANKLIN DELANO ROOSEVELT

Everyone experiences anxiety or feels panicky from time to time: the shaky knees and thudding heart, the shortness of breath, and the mind going a million kilometres per minute. Part of what keeps us alive is our ability to feel fear. In fact we are made with a kind of built-in alarm system that brings the full weight of our mental and physical prowess to bear in the face of danger—the fight or flight response.

The limbic system, the parts of the brain responsible for orchestrating our emotions, including the fight or flight response, relies on a complicated interplay between neurotransmitters and hormones to fuel the body and mind to deal with a perceived enemy.

It is however not natural to feel afraid and upset most of the time without any tangible cause. Like our immune response, our fight or flight response is meant to click into action in the face of danger and to go to rest afterwards. In our day and age, too many of us never get to relax: our minds are perpetually on high alert with the accompanying physical response.

Anxiety attack symptoms can feel awful, intense, and frightening.

The good news is that while they can seem serious, anxiety attack symptoms aren't harmful in and of themselves. Anxiety attack symptoms are *not* indications of a serious medical condition. They are simply dramatic responses to being afraid.

Common anxiety attack symptoms include:

A feeling of impending doom, that something horrible is about to happen, that you are in grave danger; a panicky feeling.
A strong feeling of fear or foreboding.
An urge to escape, to get out, to run away from danger.
Turning white, looking pale, blushing, skin blotches, turning red, burning skin.
Choking sensation, tightening throat, shortness of breath, difficulty breathing.
Tightness in the chest.
Confusion, feeling detached from reality, separate from oneself, separate from normal emotions or feeling unreal, in a dreamlike state.
Dizziness, light-headedness, unsteadiness.
Emotional upset or distress.

LIVING IN THE SPACE OF LIGHT

Fear of going crazy, of losing control, of freaking out.
Fearful thoughts that seem incessant.
Feeling a tight band around your head.
Hot or cold chills.
Inability to calm yourself down.
Tight knot in the stomach, nausea, vomiting.
Numbness, tingling sensations in any part of the body.
Plugged or stuffed ears.
Pounding or racing heart, shooting pains in the chest, neck, shoulder, head or face.
Sweating.
Trembling, shaking (visibly shaking or just trembling on the inside).
Upset stomach, an urgent desire to go to the bathroom (urinate, defecate).

This list is not exhaustive. There is a long list of anxiety symptoms. But because each body is chemically unique, anxiety affects each person differently. Consequently, anxiety symptoms vary from person to person in type or kind, number, intensity, and frequency.

The following complementary and alternative practices are currently used to treat anxiety disorders:

- Stress and relaxation techniques. When practised regularly, relaxation techniques such as mindfulness, meditation, progressive muscle relaxation, and deep breathing can reduce anxiety symptoms and increase feelings of relaxation and emotional well-being.
- Behavioural therapy.
- Postural alignment, awareness, and practice of good posture.
- Acupuncture.
- Craniosacral therapy.
- Homeopathic or naturopathic medicine, dietary supplements, or herbal products.
- Massage therapy.
- Art, music, or dance therapy.

CAARNA

- Adopt healthy eating habits. Start the day right with breakfast, and continue with frequent small meals throughout the day. Going too long without eating leads to low blood sugar, which can make you feel more anxious.
- Reduce alcohol and nicotine intake. They lead to more anxiety, not less.
- Exercise regularly. Exercise is a natural stress buster and anxiety reliever.
- Get enough sleep. A lack of sleep can exacerbate anxious thoughts and feelings, so try to get seven to nine hours of quality sleep a night.
- Medication treatment of anxiety is generally safe and effective and is often used in conjunction with therapy. Medication may be a short-term or long-term treatment option, depending on severity of symptoms, other medical conditions and individual circumstances.

Not everyone who worries a lot has an anxiety disorder. You may be anxious because of an overly demanding schedule, lack of exercise or sleep, pressure at home or work, or even from too much coffee.

The bottom line is that if your lifestyle is unhealthy and stressful, you're more likely to feel anxious. If you feel like you worry too much, take some time to evaluate how well you're caring for yourself.

- Do you make time each day for relaxation and fun?
- Are you getting the emotional support you need?
- Are you taking care of your body?
- Are you overloaded with responsibilities?
- Do you ask for help when you need it?

If your stress levels are through the roof, take control, and bring your life back into balance.

When you change the way you look at things, the things you look at change.

—WAYNE DYER

19

BE HAPPY

Happiness is not something ready made. It comes from your own actions.

—DALAI LAMA

ALTHOUGH YOU MAY have thought, as many people do, that happiness comes from being born rich or beautiful or living a stress-free life, the reality is that people who have wealth, beauty or less stress are not happier on average than those who don't enjoy those blessings.

People who are happy seem to intuitively know that their happiness is the sum of their life choices, and their lives are built on the following pillars:

Devoting time to family and friends
Appreciating what they have
Maintaining an optimistic outlook
Feeling a sense of purpose
Living in the moment

If you have been looking for happiness, the good news is that your choices, thoughts and actions can influence your level of happiness. It's not as easy as flipping a switch, but you can turn up your happiness level. Practice happiness to create a happier you.

Invest in relationships and surround yourself with happy people. Being around people who are content buoys your own mood. And by being happy yourself, you give something back to those around you. Friends and family help you celebrate life's successes and support you in difficult times. Although it's easy to take friends and family for granted, these relationships need nurturing.

Build up your emotional account with kind words and actions. Be careful and gracious with critique. Let people know that you appreciate what they do for you or even just that you're glad they're part of your life

Express gratitude in everything you do. Gratitude is more than saying thank you. It's a sense of wonder, appreciation and, thankfulness for life. It's easy to go through life without recognizing your good fortune. Often, it takes a serious illness or other tragic event to jolt people into appreciating the good things in their lives. Don't wait for something like that to happen to you. Make a commitment to practice gratitude. Each day identify at least one thing that enriches your life.

Let gratitude be the last thought before you go to sleep. Let gratitude also be your first thought when you wake up in the morning.

Cultivate optimism, practise optimism. Don't worry; choose happy. Make a conscious choice to boost your happiness. Intention is the active desire and commitment to be happy. It's the decision to consciously choose attitudes and behaviours that lead to happiness over unhappiness.

Develop the habit of seeing the positive side of things. If you're not an optimistic person by nature, it may take time for you to change your pessimistic thinking. Start by recognizing negative thoughts as you have them. Then take a step back and ask yourself these key questions:

Is the situation really as bad as I think?

Is there another way to look at the situation?

What can I learn from this experience that I can use in the future?

Foster forgiveness instead of holding a grudge and nursing grievances. It can affect physical as well as mental health, according to a rapidly growing body of research. One way to curtail these kinds of feelings is to foster forgiveness. This reduces the power of bad events to create bitterness and resentment.

Find your purpose. People who strive to meet a goal or fulfill a mission—whether it's growing a garden, caring for children or finding one's spirituality—are happier than those who don't have such aspirations. Having a goal provides a sense of purpose, bolsters self-esteem and brings people together. What your goal is doesn't matter as much as whether the process of working toward it is meaningful to you. People are seldom happier, than when they're in the "flow." This is a state in which your mind becomes thoroughly absorbed in a meaningful task that challenges your abilities. Yet it was found that the most common leisure time activity-watching watching TV—produces some of the lowest levels of happiness.

To get more out of life, we need to put more into it. Each of the flow-producing activities requires an initial investment of attention before it begins to be enjoyable." Live in the moment. Don't postpone joy waiting for a day when your life is less busy or less stressful. That day may never come. Instead, look for opportunities to savour the small pleasures of everyday life. Focus on the positives in the present moment, instead of dwelling on the past or worrying about the future. Living in the moment—also called mindfulness—is a state of active, open, intentional attention on the present. When you become mindful, you realize that you are not your thoughts; you become an observer of your thoughts from moment to moment without judging them. Mindfulness reduces stress, boosts immune functioning, reduces chronic pain, lowers blood pressure, and helps patients cope with cancer.

Money Can't Buy Happiness. Research shows that once income climbs above the poverty level, more money brings very little extra happiness.

> *"Regardless of what we achieve in the pursuit of stuff, it's never going to bring about an enduring state of happiness."*

Being happy doesn't mean that everything is perfect. It means that you've decided to look beyond the imperfections.

Happiness is a habit—cultivate it.

20

THE SOUND OF YOUR SONG

In the beginning was the word and the word was Sound.

WHEN I WAS a little girl, my mom used to whistle while she was working in the garden or when she was busy around the house. My siblings and I used to watch her with great curiosity when she did this. She made magic when she whistled her happy tunes. There used to be a silver cloud of happiness around her, which transformed the world and everyone in it. She lifted our spirits, and soon we were all laughing and playing. Everything became easy, and she completed any task she was busy with effortlessly.

My dad used to entertain children and grandchildren by belching while he said "Bulawayo." We all had to try it with him—a very masculine way to entertain small children. My mom scolded him for his unrefined behaviour and rolled her eyes. It gave us hours of pleasure as we kept on running back to him to show how we mastered the art of belching. I watched him doing this through many years, and now that he is gone I listen to my children recalling the delight it brought them, and I know any stories about him that will be carried over to next generations will never be complete without sharing his way to master the art of belching.

I love to laugh, and as a family we laugh a lot together. I can laugh myself into another dimension, and the sound coming out of my mouth then is not pretty to listen to, but it is infectious, and soon it has everyone around me in

LIVING IN THE SPACE OF LIGHT

stitches. Then none of us can stop laughing. We all laugh and cry and hold our stomachs, and in that moment we resonate with joy.

The voice is an expression of the soul. When we allow ourselves to sigh, cry, groan or moan we feel a sense of freedom because we are bypassing our control mechanism, our conscious mind that controls our speech and our voice. We facilitate self-healing when we release suppressed emotions, which are stored in our bones, muscles, tissues and organs.

The voice reflects who we truly are, it reveals our moods, fears, intentions, hopes, tensions, thoughts and desires. The sound of the voice can tell more about a person than words can ever communicate. When we allow ourselves the joy of self-expression through our voices, it awakens parts of us that may have been dormant or neglected our entire lives. We gain access to a deep inner wisdom, and with this wisdom comes transformative power.

Toning is the universal language of sound. The act of toning or tuning is the letting out of nonverbal sound as a release to create balance and harmony within self. It is achieved through the elongation of a note or tone, using breath and voice. It encourages the full spectrum of your energy field, helping to release old patterns of physical, emotional and mental limitations, allowing you to live your divine purpose more fully.

You are already toning in ways that you may not be aware of, such as: yawning when you are tired, moaning in pain, laughing when you are joyful. Other natural ways your body tones is by whistling, crying, screaming, shouting, gasping, snuffling, sneezing, belching, and so on. Studies have shown that sound enters our physical body directly before being processed by the brain, unlike vision, which must be filtered through the centre of the brain first. Sound can give us immediate access to our emotions and a deep inner body knowing.

We are all part of an orchestra. Everything in existence is a unique instrument, emitting its own particular set of notes. Each song contributes to a symphony of all that has ever existed and exists now. Each living thing that has now passed on has left an imprint in that symphony, its own set of notes, added its own movement to the larger composition, influencing the other notes and movements that have descended from its line.

There is a "song" that everything seen and unseen sings and it is a very important part of the larger symphony of existence. Take away that song, warp it, and tell that song it has to be something else or silence it and the symphony of all is incomplete. If you sabotage it, tell it it's not enough, hide it, berate it, abuse it, warp it to sound more like another's song or ignore it, you are removing an important harmony in the symphony of cosmic wholeness. It does not sound right. It is incomplete. Not whole.

Take note of your own spontaneous toning, whether it is through laughter or singing, belching or whistling, or whatever sound you use to liberate your voice and soul. Use it with consciousness of the process of breaking barriers and release. It is a clue to find the song of your soul.

The tone of the voice is more important than the words we use to communicate. The tone reflects our true intention whether it is expressed or suppressed. The voice reveals our character and personality. Our voice remembers what we have forgotten through conscious or unconscious suppression of our painful memories of experiences. Sound has a powerful ability to break through barriers, through crystallisations of thought forms, belief systems and penetrate the subconscious mind and release these blockages, even physical blockages.

Everything that has happened to you in your life culminate in the tone and the pitch of your voice and most of what we say is delivered by the tone of the voice. Our emotions are contained in the vibration of the voice. When we listen to a person's voice it may attract, repel or manipulate us. It can give us a feeling of release or excitement and we respond to it on an intuitive, emotional level. The voice tells us where we are at, mentally, emotionally and spiritually.

We resonate from our diaphragm, chest, heart, lungs, throat, tongue, and face vibrating all levels of our being connecting us with our emotions. This helps to open the heart and get out of the head, unifying our body/mind. It is more difficult to stay in a low energy state than it is to stay at a higher vibration. Using sound, for instance by singing, allows our breath to deepen, our emotions to open and the sound vibrations to move and resonate through us rather than being held back. As our breath deepens we increase the life force

LIVING IN THE SPACE OF LIGHT

within our auditory system and us and internal awareness process becomes more sensitive.

Sound shapes the universe as sound is a vibration, a frequency and we now know from quantum physics that the whole universe, including our physical bodies are made up of energy fields and technically vibrational fields of energy. Sound is vibration, specific frequencies.

Pythagoras said, "A stone is frozen music."

He demonstrated that the right sequence of sounds, played musically on an instrument, could change behaviour patterns and accelerate the healing process.

In the 1960's a Swiss scientist Dr. Hans Jenny, demonstrated how sound shapes matter.

Dr Jenny placed sand granules on to a metal plate and then played a few bars of notes from composers such as Mozart and Bach. The sand granules formed constant shapes to the vibration of the sound, and extraordinary patterns were observed.

Jenny then went further with his observation, saying that sound has a direct influence on our human biology and thus influences our health. This is because every cell in our body has its own vibrational frequency. Human cells are composed of atoms and molecules that resonate according to their mutual harmonies. Many cells together form tissues and organs that are part of a biological system. This system then vibrates according to new harmonies.

From these researches we can say that sound sculpts us. All our tissues, organs, bones and cells are made up of sound. We are held together by sound as each part of our body has its own sonic frequencies, which travel and pulsate like a wave, in an inhaling and exhaling breath.

Scientist Fabien Maman has done extensive research in music and sound and has proven that the voice has the ability to bring us into what he calls our crystal-clear self. Our voice is as unique as our fingerprints. Our voice has a soul print that we have been trying to come into contact with since birth. Our voice signifies our whole story, our make as well as our origins.

As emotions affect our body's chemical structure, we are called to learn how to balance our emotional body by using our own voice as a self-healing modality. Dissonant sounds, for example are an excellent conductor for bringing us into contact with the emotional body, as well as releasing any false beliefs and negative programming.

Our grief and anger for example, that are not expressed, cause illnesses and blockages. If we are able to release it by using our voice, we are in fact, releasing that pain and blockage in our body.

The human voice is one of the most powerful tools available to humankind. Every word we speak carries the tone of our sound as an instrument of communication and self-healing. Understanding how to tune and use this instrument effectively shifts not only our own consciousness, but also of those who receive or hear our sounds.

Sound is a powerful tool for healing and transformation, and it is much more powerful and effective when we are using our very own voice instead of to just listening to music alone. When we use our own voice, we are accessing our direct source of power, our suppressed emotions and the essence of our soul. Using other people's voices or sounds, as therapeutic as it may be, would not have the same organic effect.

Our voice is our natural source of power and liberation because it helps us to remember and recognize our true nature in the struggle of our human experience. Our voice longs to be explored with trust, love and acceptance of what we are here to experience in our life.

Sound penetrates the cells of the body, the conscious and the unconscious mind, the seen and the unseen. It can travel across space and time. Sound is powerful, yet gentle and effective and has the power to correct any condition, because it is a vibration.

The human being longs to fully open up the throat chakra, to communicate the truth and come into mastery of self-expression. There is a cry, a call deep within our hearts that wants to be heard. There is a longing for the liberation of the voice and soul—in this way to re-discover the grandeur of who we truly are—a force of the highest vibration and creation.

In a few indigenous cultures the importance of the unique melody of each soul is well known. It is sung at the moment of birth and death of a person as well as in other crucial moments and rites of passage of their life. In the

LIVING IN THE SPACE OF LIGHT

ancient thought the name or the song of a being or of an object is the being or the object. It is the vibratory nature of things revealing itself in an acoustic form.

The repetition of a mantra, the litanies of the Sufis, Gregorian chants, the use of Tibetan singing bowls on the Himalaya and of the lyre in Greece, the modern tuning forks tuned to ancient harmonic intervals, the modern electronic equipment of Hans Jenny and Royal Rife are all examples of how the power of sound has always been used to "tune" the individual to the Whole.

Music resonates within the human spirit. At the heart of humanity is a song of the soul. The spiritual significance of music can transcend communities, cultures, and creeds.

Sound (as well as thought) has the ability of actually changing the molecular structure of water. The experiments conducted by Masaru Emoto clearly demonstrate the link between the vibration of sound and the arrangement of the molecules in this extraordinary element, which is capable of storing information.

Laughter is a mechanism everyone has, laughter is part of universal human vocabulary. There are thousands of languages, hundreds of thousands of dialects, but everyone speaks laughter in pretty much the same way.

Everyone has the capacity to laugh. Children born deaf and blind are able to laugh. Babies laugh long before they acquire speech. Laughter is primitive, an unconscious vocalization. In laughter we emit sounds and express emotions that come from deep within our biological being. Whether you snort, cackle, chortle, or have a wild, weird little giggle, you have a "laugh print," a personal signature that's uniquely you.

Laughter is so basic to humans, we barely notice it, but laughter has power—the power to energise the humdrum, to add levity to the everyday nonsense. Laughter carries such a social connection that it's a mating ritual, a way to bond.

Laughter is a powerful antidote to stress, pain and conflict. Nothing works faster or more dependably to bring your mind and body back into balance than a good laugh. Humour lightens your burdens, inspires hopes, connects you to others, and keeps you grounded, focused, and alert.

— 161 —

CAARNA

Laughter gives you the courage and strength to find new sources of meaning and hope. Even in the most difficult of times, a laugh—or even simply a smile—can go a long way toward making you feel better.

Laughter really is contagious—just hearing laughter primes your brain and readies you to smile and join in the fun. Be more spontaneous. Humour gets you out of your head and away from your troubles.

Let go of defensiveness. Laughter helps you forget judgments, criticisms, and doubts.

Release inhibitions. Your fear of holding back and holding on are set aside.

Express your true feelings. Deeply felt emotions are allowed to rise to the surface.

Laughter is your birth right, a natural part of life that is innate and inborn. Infants begin smiling during the first weeks of life and laugh out loud within months of being born. Even if you did not grow up in a household where laughter was a common sound, you can learn to laugh at any stage of life.

Smiling is the beginning of laughter. Like laughter, it's contagious. When you look at someone or see something even mildly pleasing, practice smiling.

Count your blessings.

When you hear laughter, move toward it.

Spend time with fun, playful people.

Bring humour into conversations.

Laugh at yourself.

Attempt to laugh at situations rather than bemoan them.

Surround yourself with reminders to lighten up.

Keep things in perspective. Many things in life are beyond your control—particularly the behaviour of other people. While you might think taking the weight of the world on your shoulders is admirable, in the long run it's unrealistic, unproductive, unhealthy, and even egotistical.

Laughter makes you feel good and the good feeling that you get when you laugh remains with you even after the laughter subsides. Humour helps you keep a positive, optimistic outlook through difficult situations, disappointments and loss. With so much power to heal and renew, the ability to laugh easily and frequently is a tremendous resource for surmounting problems, enhancing your relationships and supporting both physical and emotional health.

There is a Traditional West Africa Griot story that says when a Tribal woman knows she is pregnant, she goes in to the wilderness with friends to pray and meditate until they hear the song of the child. They recognize that every soul has its own vibration that expresses its unique flavour and purpose. When the women attune to the song they sing it out loud. Then they return and teach it to everyone else.

When children are born into the tribe, the village community gathers and sings its song, one unique melody for each unique child. Later when children begin their education, the village again gathers to chant each child's song. They sing upon the initiation of adulthood and at the time of their marriage. If at any time someone commits a crime or aberrant social act, the villagers will circle the individual and chant their song. They recognize that the proper correction is love and the remembrance of identity. When you recognize your own song you have no desire or need to do anything that would hurt another. Finally when the soul is about to pass from this world, family and friends gather at the bedside, as they did at birth, and sing the person to the next life.

"A friend is someone who knows the song in your heart and can sing it back to you when you have forgotten the words." - C.S. Lewis.

A true friend is one that knows our song and sings it to us when we have forgotten it.

> *Life always reminds us when we are and when we are not in tune with yourself. When we feel good, we are matching our song. If we just keep singing, we will find our way home. In true end, we shall all recognize our song and sing it well.*

> —JILL MATTSON

Through the music of the sacred…through the ancient song of the earth, through the mystic rhythm of life, my voice and sound became my sanctuary of eternal existence…When I sing I pray, when I pray I

CAARNA

sing, when I sing I am one with the earth and sky, through my voice I feel one with God, through my voice I connect with each beautiful soul, through my voice I wish to give and receive infinite love.

Through my voice I am one with you…Through sound we are one. Through intention, that sound becomes sacred medicine. Through the sacred we embrace God and life. Through life we are blessed of being the music of the Universe. Through music we give and receive more love. Through love we are free and infinite!

—Daniela de Mari

21

PLANT THE GARDEN OF YOUR SOUL

WHAT ARE YOUR goals and dreams for a joyous future? What makes you happy? What are the magical qualities that you wish to live with?

Nothing is too large for you to dream and to manifest a joy-filled life. Let your imagination soar. Dream big. Plan the garden of your soul so you can surround yourself with colour and beauty. Gift yourself with fields of energy that will enhance your life.

Use geometry in the layout and pathways to put you on a road of discovery where you can practise balance and harmony that will bring miracles into your life.

Plan the garden of your soul so you can avoid the old patterns of thought and action that bring chaos and drama into your life, those that lead nowhere.

Prepare the soil of your garden with love and gratitude as you pour your heart into the project of life. Respect every ingredient of the soil as being perfect and necessary to fertilise your garden.

Plant the seeds of strength, courage, and faith throughout to give structure and form. Wait with patience to see the seeds of your dreams come to fruition.

Harmony, happiness, health, well being, prosperity, and so much more are your birth right. You do not have to beg or plead; just reach out with worthiness, sons and daughters of the King!

Observe behaviours and patterns that can upset the growth and flowering of your garden. Weed the garden with love and guard against everything that will intrude and drain the garden of life force.

Watch the blooming of your garden with gratitude and a sense of wonder. Stop to smell the roses with the sun at your back and the wind playing gently through your hair. Touch the soft and delicate petals, and feel the opening of your heart when you breathe in the love, light, and beauty of this world.

Allow love, gratitude, and positive thoughts and words to charge the waters of this world to become beautiful sacred crystals in our rivers and oceans, our dams and lakes, our water reservoirs and pipes, and our bodies too.

Take responsibility for every element in your garden, for the soil, the seeds, the water that gives life, the growth, the weeds, and the pests—all are there for you to learn the best way to tend to the garden of your soul.

Be happy. Sing and dance as you walk through the labyrinth of life. Embrace each golden moment because it is filled with infinite potential to create miracles. That is how we will bring heaven to earth.

REFERENCE

1. http://www.masaru-emoto.net/english/water-crystal.html

   Dr Masaro Emoto on human consciousness and water. https://fractalen-lightenment.com/ | FractalEnlightenment.com

2. "Trefil, James S. 1938–." Contemporary Authors, New Revision Series. . *Encyclopedia.com.* 26 Jul. 2017 <http://www.encyclopedia.com>.

3. The Hundredth Monkey by Ken Keyes Jr.

4. Michael Teal: http://www.writerscafe.org/profile/oldman
   http://www.librarything.com/profile/theoldman
   http://www.youtube.com/arrobliow

5. New stories and new processes that outline the fourth stage of awakening of ho'oponopono Author Joe Vitale's previous book, *Zero Limits*, presented a unique self-help breakthrough focused

6. Sacred Geometry: Deciphering the code by Stephen Skinner

7. Earth Grids:

   Ley Lines and Earth Energies: A Groundbreaking Exploration of the Earth's Natural Energy and How It Affects Our by David R. Cowan (Author), Chris Arnold (Author), David Hatcher Childress (Foreword)

   Bethe Hagens: www.missionignition.net/bethe
   Grid and Cells by Gordon-Michael Scallion

   Muntidimensional Griding. Article and graphics created by Deja Allison

Sacred Geometry :
The Christ Grid *by Ronald L. Holt, with Julia Griffin*

8. Robert Simmons & Naisha Ahsian, *The Book of Stones* (Berkley, CA: North Atlantic Books, 2007).

[Altman, pp.] Jennifer Altman, *Gem and Stone: Jewelry of Earth, Sea, and Sky.* (San Francisco, Chronicle Books, 2012)

[Eason, pp.]Cassandra Eason, *The New Crystal Bible* (London: Carlton Books Ltd., 2010).

[Fernie, pp.] William T. Fernie, *The Occult and Curative Powers of Precious Stones* (Blauvelt, NY: Rudolph Steiner Publications, 1973).

[Gienger, pp.] Michael Gienger, *Healing Crystals* (Scotland: Earthdancer Books, 2009).

[Hall, pp.] Judy Hall, *The Crystal Bible* (Cincinnati, OH: Walking Stick Press, 2003).

[Hall 2, pp.]Judy Hall, *The Crystal Bible 2* (Cincinnati, OH: Walking Stick Press, 2009).

[Kunz, pp.] George Frederick Kunz, *The Curious Lore of Precious Stones* (New York: Dover Publications, 1971).

[Megemont, pp.] Florence Megemont, *The Metaphysical Book of Gems and Crystals* (Rochester, VT: Healing Arts Press, 2008).

[Mella, pp.] Dorothee L. Mella, *Stone Power II* (Albuquerque, NM: Brotherhood of Life, Inc., 1986).

[Melody, pp.] Melody, *Love Is In The Earth* (Wheat Ridge, CO: Earth-Love Publishing House, 1995).

[Raphaell, pp.] Katrina Raphaell, *Crystal Enlightenment* (Santa Fe, NM: Aurora Press, 1985)

[Simmons, pp.] Robert Simmons & Naisha Ahsian, *The Book of Stones* (Berkley, CA: North Atlantic Books, 2007).

9. The Spiritual Alchemist by Natalie Reid
    Spiritual Alchemy by Dr. David. G. Brenner
    Violet Flame: The Spirit Mountain Chronicle, Mt. Shasta, CA, Winter 2007 issue.

10. http://www.nataliakuna.com/creating-your-own-sacred-space.html
    What is space clearing by Karen Kingston

11. Magazines at Marquette
    Breathing ancient air – Alyssa Contreras
    Omnihealth: We breathe the breath of our ancestors – Rabia Hayek

12. The Root of Chinese Qigong, by Yang Jwing-Ming

13. Bergonzi, M. (2011). *Il sorriso segreto dell'essere.* Milano: Mondadori. Google Scholar

    Bitbol, M. (1996). *Schrödinger's philosophy of quantum mechanics.* Boston Studies in the Philosophy of Science: Kluwer.CrossRefGoogle Scholar

    Bitbol, M. (2008). Is consciousness primary? *NeuroQuantology, 6*(1), 53–72.CrossRefGoogle Scholar

Bitbol, M. (2016). À propos du point aveugle de la science. In G. Hess & D. Bourg (Eds.), *Science, conscience et environnement*. Paris: Presses Universitaires de France.Google Scholar

Bitbol, M., & Luisi, P.-L. (2011). Science and the self-referentiality of consciousness. *Journal of Cosmology, 14*, 4728–4743.Google Scholar

Chalmers, D. (1995). Facing up the problem of consciousness. *Journal of Consciousness Studies, 2*(3), 200–219.Google Scholar

Forman, R. K. C. (1999). *Mysticism mind, consciousness*. Albany: State University of New York Press.Google Scholar

Lackoff, G., & Johnson, M. (1980). *Metaphors we live by*. Chicago: University of Chicago Press.Google Scholar

Plank, M. (1931). *The Observer*, 25 January.Google Scholar

Schrödinger, E. (1931). *The Observer*, 11 January.Google Scholar

Schrödinger, E. (1964). *My view of the world*. London: Cambridge University Press.Google Scholar

Spira, R. (2008). *The transparency of things*. Salesbury: Non-Duality Press. Google Scholar

Spira, R. (2011). *Presence*. Salisbury: Non-Duality Press.Google Scholar

Thompson, E. (2015). *Waking, dreaming, being*. New York: Columbia University Press.Google Scholar

Wheeler, J. (2007). *You were never born*. Salisbury: Non-Duality Press. Google Scholar

Made in the USA
Columbia, SC
19 October 2017